ARE WE CONNECTED?

A Small Business Guide to Digital Foundations, Follow-Up, and ROI Visibility

BRITTANY P. WEBB

Built on the B10 Core Automation Method™

Copyright © 2026 ARE WE CONNECTED? by Brittany P. Webb, Britt's Creatives

All rights reserved. No part of this book may be reproduced, distributed, or transmitted in any form or by any means, including photocopying, recording, or other electronic or mechanical methods, without the prior written permission of the author, except in the case of brief quotations embodied in critical reviews and certain other noncommercial uses permitted by copyright law.

This book is provided for educational and informational purposes only. The author is not providing legal, tax, or financial advice. You are responsible for compliance with applicable laws, regulations, platform policies, and best practices in your region and industry.

Edited and assembled in collaboration with ChatGPT by OpenAI. First Edition.

Printed in the United States of America
ebook ISBN: 979-8-9994228-8-0
Paperback ISBN: 979-8-9994228-7-3

Dedication

To the small business owner who keeps showing up.

You are not behind.

You are seen. You are strong. You are resilient. You are a builder.

And this is for YOU.

Acknowledgements

To my family: thank you for living through the late nights, the ideas endlessly kept on post-its, the "just one more thing," and the seasons where the work felt invisible. Your patience, laughter, and love have been the quiet foundation under every lesson learned throughout the chapters and beyond.

To the mentors, colleagues, clients, and friends who taught me and challenged me—sometimes gently, sometimes directly—thank you. You helped sharpen the difference between what sounds good and what actually works. You reminded me that marketing isn't a frozen moment; it's a warm, trusted system.

And to God: thank You for the redirections, the resilience, and the clarity that came when I stopped trying to force the timeline. Thank You for the purpose underneath the process—and for the reminder that what I'm building is bigger than my fear.

Finally, to you—the reader—thank you for trusting me with your time. My hope is that these pages help you connect what matters, simplify what doesn't, and build foundations that are steady enough to last.

Table of Contents

Introduction 1
  PART I 5
Hold Still, Even Stop, But Secure the Wisdom 7
Before I Built My Brand Systems 11
Brand Assets Before Busywork 15
When Visibility Isn't the Problem 17
Your Offer, Simplified 23
Automation Isn't the Point 27
The Connected Path 29
The Cost of Disconnection 35
Where Attention Lands 39
Why Lead Capture Fails 43
What Happens After They Raise Their Hand 47
The Power of Staying Connected 51
Seeing What's Actually Working 55
  PART II 61
When Everything Starts Working Together 63
The System Can Hold—But You Still Have to Lead 67
Build It to Scale: SOPs, Vendors, and a Business That Doesn't Depend on You 73
Social Media Reality 79
AI Is a Tool, Not a Decision-Maker 85
Selling Across Channels Without Losing Your Mind 91
Integrations, Fees, and the Truth About "Easy" 95
Products + Backend Protection 101
  PART III 105
Trademarks and IP Without Panic 109
Publishing as Marketing 113
Money/Admin Reality 117
Small Business Grants: What They Actually Want 121
Built to Scale, Forced to Pause 127
The Busy Ecosystem Trap 133
Faith-Led Alignment 137
  About the Author 139

Introduction

Marketing isn't hard because you're not creative. It's hard because the world is loud.

Everyone is "connected"—constantly. Phones. Notifications. Endless feeds. A hundred open tabs. A dozen inboxes. You don't have a be a rocket scientist to figure out that the future of advertising isn't in print, and hasn't been for a while now. And standing out in this look at me world, is more challenging than ever. And it's only going to get worse, with in this age of AI. Consumers are overwhelmed, and business owners are overwhelmed right alongside them. So when people say, "Marketing has to be the easiest job," I know, and you know, they've never carried the weight of trying to make a business visible in a world that's already noisy. They've never tried to turn attention into trust. They've never tried to follow up while juggling payroll, customers, family, and real life.

And if you're a small business owner, you don't just feel that pressure—you live inside it. You're doing the work, running the business, making the decisions, keeping people happy, and trying to grow... while algorithms change, platforms shift, and every other ad you see or "real" person influencer being incentivized to tell you what the company wants you to hear, and reviews promising this new tool will save you time. You buy it, you log in, you feel hopeful for about five minutes, and then it starts inundating your inbox with how-to's, videos to watch, communities to join, and new features you can't use unless you unlock the next paid tier. It most likely joins the graveyard of "good ideas" you never had the bandwidth to actually implement. And if you're not careful, it gets forgotten in your monthly paid subscriptions that you keep forgetting to cancel. Not because you don't care. Because the truth is, marketing is rarely the only thing on your plate. And even of more of a reality, you probably can't remember the password for that login and will just do it later.

This book exists because small business owners deserve something better than scattered tactics. You deserve a path. A system. A way to build digital foundations that feels steady—not stressful. But before we get into anything practical, I want you to know where this comes from. Not the polished version. The real version.

I've seen marketing from the inside of a robust corporate world—where reporting existed, pipelines were visible, support teams were in place, and the business development engine had structure around it. I learned what "robust" looks like, and I learned what "lean" looks like too. Even then, with resources in play, I watched how easy it was for work to be disconnected—manual practices, scattered systems, good people doing their best, but still fighting fragmentation behind the scenes.

Then I left. The details aren't important. I just decided one day, the alignment was no longer there, and I jumped ship looking for a lifeboat… and landed in a sailboat… after a few months of soul-searching and learning to live in peace and joy again. But when I finally started peacefully sailing my own little boat, the ocean felt bigger. The options multiplied. The noise got louder. And the responsibility got personal, fast. To you, this might sound like a "Well, duh," but to me, it was more of a "What now?" There wasn't a built-in team. There wasn't a default process. There wasn't a department to catch what I missed. It was me—building, learning, adjusting, and trying to steer forward in real time.

And while this book could focus on all the operations of entrepreneurship and business ownership that I have learned so far and am continuing to learn, it is written specifically about marketing, and so I will try to stay on course. So with all my hats tipping and swapping every which way, I realized something that may sound simple, but it changed everything in how I approached marketing: marketing is both storytelling and structure. And if you're not careful, you can put a lot of time and money into a lot of different things and end up nowhere fast.

And with that, that's where we will begin.

Marketing isn't just a logo, a website, letterhead, or a post. Marketing is psychology. It's operations. It's consistency. It's follow-through. It's what helps great work get found, understood, trusted, and chosen. Storytelling is at the heart of it—no matter how big or small the company—but storytelling without structure becomes noise and a direct path to never-anywhere-land. And structure without a story becomes cold. The sweet spot is when the two work together, connected.

Small businesses struggle when marketing gets treated like a creative task instead of a connected system. You end up with a little of everything and a lot of confusion. A website that doesn't convert. A Google profile that's half-finished. A social page that looks active but doesn't lead anywhere. A CRM, if one is connected, that nobody checks. An inbox full of inquiries that get a follow-up tag assigned, but the reminder keeps popping up and remind me later renewed for another day. If you're insightful and well-intentioned, you might even have a bunch of tools in your tool stack, subscribed and ready to go. But do they talk to each other? Do you still look at it all and think, "My marketing doesn't work" or "I can't tell if my marketing is even doing anything."

But what it might really mean is, "My system isn't connected."

Introduction

This book is a practical guide to building connected digital foundations—without pretending you have unlimited time, unlimited money, or a full marketing team. We're going to talk about what people don't explain enough: how attention really works right now, why clarity beats creativity when your business is small, how trust gets built without being loud or salesy, how leads get captured and followed up with consistently, and how boundaries matter—because marketing that crosses the line stops being marketing and starts feeling like spam.

You'll see B10 referenced throughout, because it's the B10 Core Automation Method™ framework inside my 12.5 Marketing System™ that keeps the work in order. Not because you need more complexity—because you need less. B10 isn't about doing everything. It's about simplifying and connecting what matters, in a way you can actually maintain. And because platforms and policies change fast, we're leaning on principles that hold steady: clarity, consent, trust, proof, follow-through, and visibility into what's working.

I'm not here to claim I can fix every business. I'm here to help you spot what may be disconnected, so you can stop guessing and start making intentional moves — whether you DIY it, use AI, ask a friend, or hire the right expert. I hope the lessons I learned (sometimes the hard way) help you grow, scale, and build with more peace along the way.

This isn't about hype. It's about building something you can keep.

So before we start—take a breath. If you've been overwhelmed, you can get grounded. You can get focused. You can find a clear path. You can get connected.

Let's build it.

Are We Connected?

PART I

Foundations of Connection

CHAPTER 1
Hold Still, Even Stop, But Secure the Wisdom

Before we go any further, here's a question worth asking: if someone found you today, would they know exactly what to do next after reading "Jump Ship, Secure the Wisdom"?

I learned when to hold still. Even stop. Not when I had to necessarily—but when discernment pressed on my heart and my head and alignment no longer serves me. To continue would cost me more than stopping. And that is one of the most challenging decisions to make for myself. It doesn't always seem black and white. There seems to be a crossroads. A what if that speaks so loudly. But if you sit with it, and for me I met it with prayer, it will reveal the path. And sometimes it's not the one you hoped it would be.

I learned this the hard way. My first experience with taking an idea and trying to build it into a business—yeah, it failed. Well, that's not true. My first, first, idea was a boutique in my little town. I wanted to open it in our family's office location. It was a perfect location. I wanted to name it City Mouse Country Mouse after one of my favorite Golden Books from when I was little. My husband is as country as it gets. And I would say that I was a city girl in a country world for a long time, although I have accepted and embraced the country lifestyle as I have lived here now longer than I haven't. I wanted to bring in his and hers fashion, curated sundries, and local finds. I thought that would be so fun. But, a logo was all I got done in that venture before we became pregnant with our third child, and it was just a vision of the past as I quickly was tending to the needs of three beautiful, healthy children under five years old.

So, my second idea, but really my first experience, came from a real-world need. My daughter, at three years old, got to pick her first pair of glasses. If you've ever shopped children's glasses with prescription lenses, they are not cheap. We thought we were making the responsible investment by limiting her choice to the ones claiming to be more durable. The only problem was, they were the ones she absolutely didn't want—because they didn't have pizazz. So as parents, we overrode her decision with practicality as our deciding factor, and when they arrived, she wouldn't wear them. Yay! She won. But what you don't know about me, is that I don't like to lose when there is a reason we are playing. And the reason she needed the glasses was greater than her desire to like her glasses.

So, my problem-solver hat came out. I walked in the house holding this very expensive new pair of glasses as my daughter made her way upstairs, adamant that she was not wearing those. I know, even at three, I could tell that I had a beautiful, strong-willed, little mini-me God gave me to raise. I made my way to my craft desk and started pulling out supplies. What do I have? How can I make this work? I pulled out my "sparkles" from my something blue I added to my sister-in-law's heels, with her permission of course, for our wedding day, and held them up in the air like in The Grinch, when he has an idea! My husband looked over at me, I'm certain the expression on his face was from the thought "What in the world are you getting ready to do?" and I calmly asked him to trust me, and I got out some epoxy and I sparkled Addie's glasses.

SparkleAddies. Cute right?

When she saw them, her eyes lit up. She was excited. I didn't even have to ask her to wear them. Not a fight. Slipped those suckers over her head, pulled her hair up around the band, and off she went. Just a big, proud smile. Whew! That could have gone a couple different ways, with both my daughter and my husband. But it was a win in my book. And based on that reaction, my assessment was that surely this could bring confidence to so many kids, so the wheels started turning in my head.

I created a logo, partnered with her eye care team to provide the SparkleAddies service, submitted and got awarded a trademark, and built a Wix website. It was well received and I was excited... until they started coming back wanting the stones put back on.

And suddenly, I had a new problem to solve—one I had no idea was about to turn into an uphill battle.

I worked late into the night, night after night—often past 3:00 a.m.—testing adhesives, finishes, and methods that sound brilliant when you're tired and determined. I experimented with a drill press with endless drill bits, and even techniques like hydrodipping. I looked into partnering with brands like Jibbitz to see if I could get something small enough to attach safely for children. I was chasing one repeatable process that would finally make it scalable—clean, consistent, and without returns.

Swarovski crystals covered my brick floor, glittering like confetti. I frequently had epoxy on my hands, there were drill bits and tweezers left around everywhere, and prototypes stacked like proof that I wasn't "playing business." I tried everything I could think of. I consulted with engineers and experienced R&D managers. New approaches felt like they might finally make the whole thing click—but didn't. I kept believing I was one tweak away from a breakthrough.

But the part I later found out—from the owner of the glasses manufacturer themselves, as we stood behind a table together at a conference in Ohio with my SparkleAddies with his prestigious brand—was that the material was designed to resist exactly what I needed as a result one pair would turn out great; the next would fail. I couldn't control the elements surrounding the inconsistent outcomes. And when I say I believe I tried everything, I felt it to my core. The blood, sweat, tears—and dollars—I put into research and development for this project were too many to want to stop. But with this new information, I couldn't just ignore it.

And even though that day behind that table together, I almost secured a partnership with the big glasses manufacturer, but something eerie about the timing sat heavy on my heart, and I couldn't go through with it. Just following, our sample embarked on a long sail overseas for pricing for our own mold, colors, styles, stones already inlaid in the material. Not wanting to give up, I almost signed the proposal. It would have left us with an astronomical quantity sitting in our garage. And ultimately, it was still "almost figured out." And almost wasn't sure enough for me to invest what it would taken to take the next step.

So I made the really hard, grown-up decision: I held still. I stopped. I packed it up into boxes. Hard to believe that an idea that big could fit into just a few boxes, but it did. I shut the closet door and steered clear for a while. It was a hard failure I didn't want to look at.

Years later, when I finally opened that closet again, I dropped to the floor and cried ugly, boohoo, crocodile tears—not because I failed, but because I had fought so hard to build something real. I envisioned all the little kids it would have boosted their confidence. Brought them joy. And helped those parents feel good about choosing the practical ones. But I tried so hard. I cared so much. And I believed I could make it happen. And I didn't.

That season didn't disappear. It trained me. It taught me how to build under pressure. How to problem-solve when the answer isn't obvious. How to respect what it takes to turn an idea into something real. How to pivot without letting the pivot become shame—but instead letting it become a crash course.

That season handed me a lot of lessons, but one in particular is going to show up in every chapter of this book: in small business, a good idea is only part of a successful business. You have to have an offer you can fulfill, and you need a system to support it—one that can survive real life.

I couldn't even get to the marketing part with SparkleAddies because I never fully got out the gate with the offer. And I believe if I could have, the storytelling would have been captivating and fun to market. But that wasn't in God's plan for me—and everything I've done since has grown from that foundation.

A good story has power. It doesn't have to be loud, the biggest, the prettiest, or have the strongest punch line. It just has to be true and land.

Long before algorithms and ad managers, connection started the same way: someone tells a story and people lean in.

I've watched my husband do this his whole life. He can take a normal moment and turn it into a room-connector—not because he's performing, but because his stories have timing, honesty, and warmth. People relax. They laugh. They remember. They want more. He truly has a gift.

And that's the part small business owners forget when marketing feels like a checklist. The goal isn't to post more. It's to create a moment where someone quietly thinks, "I trust this person. I want to know what they are selling. I want to buy from them."

In this book, we'll talk workflows and follow-up and visibility. But every tool only works when it's carrying something human—and when it's connected to a system that doesn't collapse the moment life gets busy.

Keep this in mind: when your systems connect, your business gets quieter—and you get steadier. Next: "Before I Built My Brand Systems".

CHAPTER 2
Before I Built My Brand Systems

You can be doing a lot and still feel stuck, sometimes looking back wondering where you even started. Or like my over 40 brain likes to give me a good ole pause, and then, "Wait, what was I doing again?". That's why I built my method. My systems. It's about simplifying and focusing. It isn't about doing more—it's about making the next step obvious. Sure, you can add bells and whistles. Believe me, I'm a glitz and glimmer kind of gal. But you can easily get hung up on all the details and forget where the throughline is. The core that makes it connect and brings it home.

After my failing forward from the SparkleAddies venture, I saw the other side. The side of marketing from an established company, on a corporate-level, and ready to grow and expand. I had the honor of starting and developing their marketing department. I spent nearly seven years there sharing many successes with the team. And then not as suddenly as one might hope, I made a bold pivot. Not because I was pushed—because I knew staying would cost me more than leaving. And it was time.

It wasn't dramatic the way people assume it should be. It was quieter than that. It was the decision that feels like obedience. Like integrity. Like, "I can't unsee what I see." And then came the messy middle—the building, the pivoting, the learning, the making it up as I went, with a mix of grit, ChatGPT, and God.

Leaving something stable, something established, something impressive on paper that I had earned was really tough. And I'm not going to lie, it set me back. And for a while, I felt like I was floating in the middle of the ocean with a resume I didn't think I would need in one hand and a prayer in the other.

When I try to explain that season, the words don't come easily. Emotion still floods in first. The closest metaphor I have is this: it felt like stepping—no, jumping—off a yacht, hoping to find a lifeboat, and eventually landed in something smaller, lighter, and unfamiliar. A sailboat. You're still moving forward, the peace blowing like wind in your hair… but then it hits you. How do you drive the boat? Where are you going? What do you do first? And how do you find the right people to connect with again?

I had tried building a business before. I got close enough to taste it, and it turned into an expensive lesson. But by the time I stepped into buying my next LLC with the state, I had also experienced other businesses on the inside. They had a compelling offer, they were talented, and they weren't

Are We Connected?

for me. I was certain that for this season, this next chapter, it would have to be mine.

As I reflected on the past businesses, I had been a part of, I realized a few things. They were of course larger than anything I had built on my own. Had processed, people, and positioning that I didn't. And even with all that—there was still disconnection.

Sometimes it was disconnection from customers, where the business was busy but the follow-through felt thin. Sometimes it was disconnection inside the systems themselves—things living in different places, data split across tools, no clean visibility into what was working and what wasn't. Sometimes it was messaging that changed depending on who touched it last. And honestly, they were okay with it. Some of them even thought it was a clean, simple system but when a new person comes in and they get onboarded, it is anything but simple and streamlined. The digital foundation part of their marketing wasn't a priority the way other parts were. For them, it worked. Maybe it always would. And maybe it wouldn't. Only time will tell.

But small businesses don't get that same cushion.

In a small business, disconnection becomes a liability the moment the owner becomes the glue holding all the pieces together. You're not just the visionary—you're the reminder system. You're the follow-up. You're the customer service department. You're the marketing department. You're the IT department when something breaks. You're the finance tracker. You're the social media scheduler. You're the "Did we reply to that?" person. And after a while, that level of mental load doesn't just make you tired—it starts to make you resentful of your own business.

What I didn't understand until my rebuild season was how easy it is, once you see the noise, to swing to extremes. Once you realize the internet is loud and attention is expensive, it becomes tempting to do one of two things.

One is to hustle harder—post more, try everything, grab every new platform, buy every tool, hope something finally sticks. The other is to shut down—decide marketing is "not your thing," go back to word-of-mouth and prayer, and tell yourself you'll figure it out later when life slows down.

I get both impulses. I really do. I've lived them.

But neither one builds a connected business.

Because connection isn't built through panic, and it isn't built through avoidance. Connection is built through a steady system—one that simplifies your digital life, makes follow-up consistent, and gives you visibility without making you carry the whole thing in your head or on post-it notes and phone reminders. And if you've ever felt like you're drowning in tabs, logins, half-finished tools, and good intentions… that doesn't mean you're failing. It means you've outgrown disconnected marketing.

And that's where the real work begins.

Here's what matters: clarity isn't a personality trait. It's something you build on purpose. Next: "Brand Assets Before Busywork".

CHAPTER 3

Brand Assets Before Busywork

I remember realizing that brand assets before busywork wasn't a "someday" problem—it was a right-now one, because real life doesn't pause long enough for you to catch up.

The first place most small businesses skip—because they want to "get moving"—is the part that saves the most time later: brand assets.

And I get why. Brand work feels like the "soft" stuff when you're staring at real responsibilities. You want customers. You want sales. You want movement. So you rush past the foundation and start building on whatever you have—an old logo, a color you kind of like, a font that looked good on somebody else's website, a Canva file you can't find again, a login you're pretty sure you used once. It's not because you're careless. It's because you're trying to survive. Just get something and go.

But inconsistency costs time, money, and credibility in ways that doesn't show up immediately. It shows up later as confusion. Later as rework. Later as "Why does this look different everywhere?" Later as paying someone again to recreate what you already paid for once. Later as a business that looks busy but still doesn't feel clear.

So before you touch a social page, a website, an ad, a business page, or a chamber membership, you want to lock in the assets that keep you from rebuilding every season. Not because you're trying to be fancy, but because you're trying to be steady, timeless, and decisive. This is also where the 12.5 Marketing System™ with Branding.

At minimum, you need a primary logo and a simplified version. You need light and dark variations so your branding doesn't fall apart depending on whether the background is white or dark. You need a high-resolution PNG with a transparent background so you can actually place your logo without that ugly white box around it. And if you plan to print anything—signage, packaging, embroidery, a banner, a vehicle decal—you need a vector file (SVG, EPS, or AI) so your brand scales cleanly without turning into pixelated regret.

This is one of those moments where small business owners think they're "saving money" by skipping it, but they're really just pushing the cost into the future. And future-you always pays more. Pays more in frustration. And time.

If you want to take one more step that will make you feel like a real business owner in the best way, create a simple one-page brand guide.

Nothing fancy. Just your fonts, your logo rules, and your colors recorded in the formats you'll eventually need. Your hex colors represented with a # and your RGB for screens and CMYK for print. Having both used in the appropriate places will ensure that your "same color" will show up consistently across a website, a flyer, and a shirt. That's how people end up chasing their own tail trying to match something they thought was already decided.

If you can't find your logo files in ten seconds, you don't have brand assets—you have brand stress. And most small businesses don't realize how much time they bleed by rebuilding the same basics over and over: resizing, re-coloring, re-making, re-matching, re-explaining.

So let this be the line in the sand. Get the logo variations. Get the transparent PNGs. Get the vector file. Write down your colors and fonts in one place. Not because you're trying to be fancy—because you're trying to be consistent without working harder than you already are.

Because once your assets are locked, you stop reinventing your business every time you need to show up.

And then the next question becomes simple: now that you look like a real business, do people understand what you actually do—fast? That's where we're going next.

CHAPTER 4

When Visibility Isn't the Problem

Here's the myth: when visibility isn't the problem is only for people who are already 'together.' The truth is, it's what helps you become together without losing your mind.

Most small business owners don't struggle with visibility the way they think they do. They struggle with what happens after someone notices them.

This is one of the hardest truths to accept when you're doing "all the right things." You've posted. You've updated your website. You've shared your story. You've told people what you do. You've even paid for ads, boosted a post, hired help at some point. And still, the business feels inconsistent. Leads come in waves. Conversations start, but they don't always turn into customers. People say, "I keep seeing you everywhere," but that recognition doesn't translate into steady momentum.

That's usually the moment when business owners assume they need more visibility. More posting. More platforms. More reach. More noise.

But visibility without connection is just exposure. It looks active, but it doesn't move anything forward.

I learned this long before I ever had language for it.

In corporate environments, visibility is rarely the issue. People recognize the brand. They know what the company does at a high level. What matters more is what happens behind the scenes—how interest is tracked, how conversations are logged, how follow-up happens, how opportunities move from one stage to the next. There's a system carrying the weight so individuals don't have to rely on memory, mood, or heroics to keep things moving.

When I stepped into entrepreneurship, I assumed that once I had enough visibility, the rest would naturally fall into place. I knew how to tell stories. I knew how to build trust in person. I knew how to communicate. What I underestimated was how quickly things fall apart when there isn't a clear path underneath the attention.

It's one thing to have someone stop scrolling. It's another thing to know where they land, what happens next, and how they're supported without you having to chase the interaction down.

In small business, the owner often becomes the bridge between interest and action. You're the follow-up. You're the reminder. You're the one who remembers who asked about pricing, who wanted to book later, who said "check back next month," who DMed instead of emailed, who filled out the form but never replied. That works when your business is small and your mental load is manageable. It stops working the moment life happens. And all the sudden you can't take a vacation because you're a "dancing bear", and if you stop dancing, it all stops. And you can't let that happen.

This is where the disconnect starts to cost you more than money. It costs you energy.

I've watched business owners get frustrated with themselves for not being "better at marketing," when the truth is they were doing too much manually for too long. They weren't failing. They were overfunctioning—holding everything together with good intentions and exhaustion.

And the market doesn't reward exhaustion.

The irony is that many small businesses are more visible than they've ever been, but less supported than they've ever felt. They're posting into the void, answering messages at night, juggling inboxes, and trying to remember which conversation belongs where. When someone finally reaches out, it feels urgent. When they don't respond right away, it feels personal. When leads go cold, it feels like rejection.

That emotional weight is rarely acknowledged in marketing conversations, but it matters. Because when everything depends on you, marketing stops feeling like growth and starts feeling like pressure.

This is where my sailboat season taught me something I couldn't learn any other way. When you're running lean, you don't have the luxury of wasted motion. You don't get to try everything. You learn quickly what actually matters. You learn which steps create momentum and which ones just make you feel busy. You learn that simplicity isn't a downgrade—it's survival.

I started asking different questions. Not "How do I get more eyes?" but "What happens when someone finds me?" Not "How do I look more established?" but "How do I respond faster, cleaner, and more consistently?" Not "What tool should I buy next?" but "What problem am I actually trying to solve?"

I saw the same pattern in client work, too—sometimes in ways that were almost tender, because it wasn't laziness or lack of passion. It was disconnection.

I remember one client meeting me in the lobby of an office that wasn't mine and wasn't hers. She walked in carrying bags—literal bags—stuffed with fabric samples, sketches, and handwritten notes. She had done some homework somewhere on a computer, but everything she brought to me was penciled out like a dream she didn't want to lose. She was excited. She was motivated. She was certain she needed a Shopify store.

And Shopify does feel like a finish line. A storefront. A launch. A moment you can announce. But when I asked a few grounding questions, the gaps showed up fast. She hadn't registered her business with the state yet. No EIN. No business bank account. She didn't have a clear product list—sizes, colors, variations. No photos ready. No packaging plan. No shipping plan. No clear ICP. Side note: everyone is not an ICP—if you build something for everyone, you're building it for no one at all. She didn't have a computer, and she relying on the hope of a virtual assistant to manage orders—which may have actually been a viable solution, but she would still need some way to connecting processes "virtually" with them. When I asked if she could send me product pictures, she told me she could mail items to me and have them delivered to my mailbox.

Quick definition, because I use this shorthand a lot: ICP means your Ideal Customer Profile—the specific kind of person or business you can help best, the one you're most equipped to serve without bending into a pretzel. And the guardrails I'm setting up here are simple: we pick one primary ICP, we write to them first, we build one clean path from "interested" to "next step," and we don't add new platforms until the current path is working.

Then we got to payments. She wanted to accept checks. Did not want to set up a table at local community events.

And none of that made her dream wrong. It just made the sequence and the possibility of system very disconnected and *virtually* impossible without the working use of a phone or computer that could run her online store dream.

That was the moment I knew I couldn't take the project on as a build. The budget was minimal, so for a time, I consulted instead, and I told her the truth with care: her next best step wasn't Shopify. I suggested an Etsy store, a simple brand foundation, and a path forward she could actually maintain until she was ready for something bigger. But she had many steps to conquer before we entered into an online space. Because connection isn't just about being online. It's about being ready to receive what online attention brings.

That story sticks with me because it shows what I've seen over and over again: you can be connected in one area of your life and disconnected in another. Marketing exposes the disconnect, not because you're failing, but because the internet amplifies whatever isn't supported underneath.

Sometimes the disconnect is operational. Sometimes it's logistical. And sometimes it's ownership.

I can't tell you how many times I've opened a small business website and felt the owner's stress before I ever read a sentence. Ten menu tabs. Multiple phone numbers. Broken links. A pop-up asking me to subscribe before I even know what they do. A contact form that goes to an inbox nobody checks. Or the most painful one: a website that technically exists, but the owner can't update it, can't access it, and doesn't even know who controls the login.

That's not a visibility problem. That's a handoff problem.

And handoff is where small businesses leak opportunity.

A website isn't just a prettier version of your business card. It's the place where attention turns into action—where someone goes when they're ready to stop watching and start deciding. And if that place is confusing, outdated, slow, or impossible for you to manage, you don't just lose leads—you lose trust.

This is why Websites—Digital Foundations is Phase 2 in the 12.5 Marketing System™. Because your website is the home base of connection. It's where your offer gets clarified, your next step gets simplified, and your follow-up stops depending on you remembering who said what and when.

Visibility can open the door, but your website decides whether people walk in—or quietly back out.

And you see the cracks in the foundation fast—when someone fills out a form and nothing happens for days. You feel it when a DM sits unanswered because it came in during dinner or practice or bedtime. You experience it when you circle back later and wonder if too much time has passed. Slowly, without realizing it, you start believing the story that marketing doesn't work.

What's really not working is the path.

Connection isn't about being everywhere. It's about making sure that when someone raises their hand—even quietly—you're ready for them. It's about reducing friction so the next step is obvious, supported, and repeatable. It's about building a system that assumes you're human, not perfect.

That's what eventually shaped the B10 Core Automation Method™—Phases 3-12 of the 12.5 Marketing System™. Not because I wanted to create a framework, but because I needed a way to stop bleeding energy. I needed a way to protect follow-through without becoming a machine. I needed marketing to support my life, not consume it.

If Chapter 1 was the reality check, and Chapter 3 was about building a foundation you don't have to rebuild every season, this chapter is the hinge: attention isn't enough. Visibility is the invitation. Connection is the relationship. And without a system to support the relationship, marketing becomes a performance instead of a process.

As we move forward, everything we build will come back to this principle: attention is borrowed, but trust is earned. And trust is built through consistency, clarity, and follow-through—not volume.

So if you've ever felt like you're doing a lot and still not seeing results, this isn't a call to do more. It's an invitation to do fewer things better, with a connected path underneath them. That's where relief begins. And that's where growth actually starts.

The goal isn't more hustle—it's a setup that can carry you when life gets loud. Next: "Your Offer, Simplified".

CHAPTER 5
Your Offer, Simplified

If you've been showing up consistently and still feel like business is inconsistent, it might not be your visibility. It might be your offer—specifically, the way it's being explained.

After you've been in business long enough, you start to notice a pattern that messes with your confidence if you don't name it. You can be visible—posted, present, consistent, even proud of what you're putting out—and still feel like nothing is sticking. People watch. They react. They compliment. They say things like, "I love your page," or "I keep seeing you everywhere," and you take that as a sign you're finally breaking through. Then you look at your calendar, your inbox, your sales, your actual pipeline, and it's like the praise floated right past the part that pays bills.

That's when business owners do what I've done too: we assume visibility is the missing ingredient. We assume we need to do more. Post more. Share more. Show up on one more platform. Say it louder. Make it prettier. Pay for reach. Try the thing that worked for someone else. But there's another reason marketing can feel like it's not working even when you're working: your offer might not be landing. Not because your work isn't good. Not because you're not talented. Not because you're not "creative enough." The problem is usually simpler and more annoying than that: you haven't translated what you do into words a customer can understand quickly.

And right now, "quickly" matters more than we want it to. People aren't reading like they used to. They're scanning. They're multitasking. They're making decisions while standing in line, sitting in carpool, half-paying attention between work meetings, or scrolling at night with their brain already overloaded. In that kind of world, you can't build trust on a paragraph that sounds impressive but doesn't mean anything to the person reading it.

This is the part where small business owners start to feel like marketing is asking them to become someone else. You want to sound professional, so you choose professional words. You want to sound established, so you use language you've heard bigger companies use.

You want to sound legit, so you start writing things like "comprehensive solutions," and "strategic services," and "helping businesses transform," and "elevating brands." And none of those phrases are wrong.

They're just blurry.

They don't create a picture.

They don't let a customer feel the outcome. They don't answer the only question the overwhelmed person on the other end is trying to solve: What does this do for me?

I've seen this happen in every industry. It shows up in the businesses that are too humble to name what they actually deliver, and it shows up in the businesses that can deliver a lot but can't choose a simple way to say it. It also shows up in the businesses that have learned so much over time that they forget what it feels like to not know what they know. They start talking like an expert to other experts and wonder why customers don't move.

The other thing that makes offers muddy is when you have too many things you offer. You can do multiple things, so you list them all. I experienced this with my third business ownership venture, I built a Wordpress site for our social media first business I entered into with a partner. That was our initial plan, however, my service area was needing other marketing services. Having the experience that I had in my corporate role, I could perform other services, so I added those to the menu of services. This cluttered the offering and created more questions and variations of even those additional services. Ultimately, misalignment led to us parting ways and my fourth entrepreneur venture, B Creative Systems™ simplifying marketing through the 12.5 Marketing System™ with Phase 1: Branding, Phase 2: Websites, Phase 3-12 B10 Core Automation Method™, and .5 Ongoing Support with Social Media as the fuel to bring leads into the system and amplify the impacts.

That clear offering came only after I built my next Wordpress site which had more clarity in offering, but not as I began expanding my ecosystem with Prompt Therapy™ and the branded B10 app, Bline™, and Britt's Creatives.

The other side of this is when a business has grown in layers and your service list grew right along with it. You start with one thing, then you add another, then you learn another skill, then someone asks if you can do this too, and you can, so you do. Soon you've built an entire menu of work you're capable of delivering.

You've got a lot of answers, a lot of options, a lot of ways you can help—and the customer freezes.

Because too many options feels risky.

Too many services feels like a maze. And when someone is already tired, they don't want to solve a puzzle just to figure out how to work with you.

They want to feel safe.

They want to feel like the next step is obvious.

There's also a quieter reason we don't simplify—one I've had to be honest about in my own seasons. Sometimes we don't simplify because we're attached to the full story. We've worked hard. We've lived through a season. We've earned our experience the long way. We want people to see the depth. We want them to understand there's a reason we do what we do the way we do it. We want our marketing to feel like integrity, not like some watered-down version of us.

So, Hello. I'm Brittany. And I'm guilty. Hand-raised, it was me! I had a cluttered offer. I had so many pieces that made my business tick on the inside that I had built out and wanted to paint the picture for you on my website so others could understand how it all connected too. What I realized was it was way too much. My intricately detailed connections and emotionality that I assigned to my offering needed to stay in internal documents, if that, or likely they could just stay in my journal or notes app. I was way too close to it. I didn't need it all to be on my website.

When I rebranded to a Framer and Shopify Site, I simplified and streamlined the website in preparation for connection to Bline™ as our pilot agency setting up B Creative Systems™ as the Agency and Prompt Therapy™, Britt's Creatives, and clients into the app with their own Bline™ for connected visibility. Upon completion, it was like a breath of fresh air. The right things were emphasized, paths were clearer, even the complexities of the ecosystem made complete sense, now intentionally mapped properly, without adding more. Less is more marks a pivotal concept referenced often in layout and design instruction. White space speaks too, and sometimes more than well-constructed content.

The moral of the story: marketing isn't where you tell the full story first. Marketing is the doorway, not the living room. The doorway has one job: make the next step clear enough that someone feels confident walking in. That's why I keep coming back to one tool, over and over, in my own business and with clients. It's simple enough to feel insulting at first, and that's why it works: you should be able to say what you do in one sentence. Not your mission statement. Not your bio. Not a list of everything you offer—one sentence. The kind you could say out loud without feeling like you're reading a script: I help ___ get ___ by ___.

When someone can understand that sentence, they can decide whether you're for them. When they can't understand it, they might still like you, still follow you, still compliment you—and still never become a customer. Here's what it sounds like when it's clear and normal: I help busy parents get dinner on the table faster by delivering prepped meals weekly. I help homeowners protect their investment by repairing roofs before leaks spread. I help small business owners build connected digital foundations so marketing stops feeling scattered.

That sentence is not supposed to hold your entire identity. It's not the full version of your brilliance. It's the bridge. The mistake I see all the time is business owners trying to make the bridge carry the whole house. They cram everything into the sentence, then wonder why it collapses under it's own weight. The goal is not to explain everything. The goal is to make someone understand enough to keep going.

If you want to know whether your offer is too blurry, here's the test I use when I'm reading someone's website or caption and I feel my brain start to glaze over: underline every word your customer wouldn't naturally use. Then translate it into real life. If you say "comprehensive solutions," what do you actually do? If you say "digital transformation," what changes for the customer? If you say "customer engagement," are you texting, emailing, calling, automating, following up, responding faster?

Customers don't buy words. They buy outcomes. They buy relief. They buy the feeling of, "Finally—someone who gets it." Once you have the one sentence, then you earn the right to bring them into the living room. That's where your proof lives—your process, your examples, your results, your story. That's where your customer can see what working with you actually looks like and feel safe enough to commit.

But you can't skip the doorway. Because when your offer is clear, everything else gets easier. Your website mirrors it. Your social content points back to it. Your bio stops reading like a resume and starts reading like an invitation. Your call-to-action gets cleaner. Your DMs get simpler. Your follow-up gets easier because you're not trying to explain yourself from scratch every time.

Clarity isn't dumbing it down. Clarity is connection. And if you've been feeling like you're doing a lot and still not seeing the right kind of results, this is your permission slip: you don't need to be louder. You need to be easier to understand.

In the next chapter, we're going to build the path that comes after the sentence—where people land, what you capture, how you follow up, and how you keep it simple enough to maintain when real life is happening. Because the whole point of this book isn't to give you more marketing to do. It's to give you a connected way to keep doing what you already do—without losing yourself in the noise.

CHAPTER 6

Automation Isn't the Point

It's the middle of a normal day. Your phone buzzes and you think, w*as that the person who asked about pricing… or the one who said next month?

That's not a marketing problem. That's a tracking problem. And that's where automation starts to matter—not as a flex, but as relief.

Automation has a reputation, and depending on who you're talking to, it's either the magic fix that will save your business or the cold robotic thing that makes people feel like a number. When automation is done wrong, it creates distance and starts to feel like a machine that's more interested in extracting money than earning trust, which is why so many small business owners flinch at the idea of building it. But automation isn't the point—connection is—and automation is simply what protects connection when life gets busy, when your hands are full, and when follow-through can't depend on you remembering everything at exactly the right time.

Most small business marketing isn't failing because the owner isn't trying; it's failing because it's disconnected and manually held together.

Manual feels personal at first—you reply to everything yourself, track leads in your head, juggle DMs, texts, emails, and notes—but manual has a ceiling because your brain was never meant to be a CRM, your memory was never meant to be a pipeline, and your stress response was never meant to become your marketing strategy.

Messages slip, leads go cold, forms get filled out and sit unanswered, and then the owner carries the emotional weight like the disconnect is a personal failure, when the truth is it's structural, not intentional.

This is where automation becomes a form of integrity, because automation done right isn't cold—it's consistent. The best automation is almost invisible; it feels like professionalism, like someone getting a confirmation when they reach out so they're not wondering if they fell into a black hole, like clear next steps instead of vague promises, like reminders that protect both the customer's time and your capacity, and like context being stored somewhere reliable so you're not reconstructing the entire story from scattered threads. That's not spam—it's service—and in an overwhelmed world, service is how trust gets built.

The fear comes from seeing automation used as a shortcut for relationship—blasting messages without warmth, sending sequences that don't match the moment, treating volume like connection—but automation doesn't have to strip your humanity; it can carry it.

The simplest way to think about it is that every workflow has a starting point, a next step, and a rule for what happens when something changes: someone fills out a form and the next step is clear, someone books and the next step is clear, someone pays and the next step is clear, confirmation and gratitude.

You don't need a giant funnel or dozens of workflows; you need the few high-impact supports where trust breaks when the ball gets dropped, because the goal isn't to automate everything—it's to automate what drains you and quietly sabotages consistency so you can save time for what really matters in business and outside of business.

There's also a part most marketing conversations skip: your nervous system is part of the marketing system.

When you're overwhelmed and reactive, marketing becomes urgent, sporadic, and emotional, and you start making decisions from fear—buying tools you don't need, joining platforms you won't maintain, switching direction to chase relief—so automation, the way I structure it, isn't about becoming more robotic, it's about becoming more regulated.

It removes unnecessary friction, creates repeatability you can trust, and turns your marketing from chaos into rhythm, which is why the B10 isn't about stacking tools—it's about stopping the bleed of disconnected effort so your presence stays steady even when real life is loud.

So let this be the reset: automation isn't the point, connection is the point, and when you automate the right things you don't become less human—you become more present. You stop living in your inbox, you stop carrying every detail in your head, you stop apologizing for delays you didn't intend, and you start building with confidence because you're no longer cleaning up preventable messes behind the scenes; you're not building a machine, you're building a system you can breathe inside.

Remember this: confidence grows when you can see what's happening and what to do next. Next: "The Cost of Disconnection".

CHAPTER 7

The Connected Path

There was a season where I realized I was tired of guessing. Guessing whether someone was serious. Guessing whether they got my message. Guessing whether they were still interested. Guessing where they came from. Guessing what worked. Guessing if my marketing was doing anything at all.

And I'm not talking about dramatic, life-changing guesses. I'm talking about the daily ones that pile up until you feel like you're running a business with your eyes half closed. That's when marketing stops feeling like growth and starts feeling like pressure—because pressure loves uncertainty.

So I started building the opposite of guessing. Not perfection. Not a massive overhaul. Just a connected path that leaves a trail.

The B10 is that trail. It's the sequence that keeps leads from slipping and keeps outcomes from disappearing into "I think" and "maybe" and "I'm pretty sure." It's what makes follow-up calmer because you're not reconstructing the story every time. It's what makes visibility possible because you're not relying on memory to do analytics.

And once you understand it as a path, you can build it in pieces without getting overwhelmed—starting with the moment someone reaches out, and ending with the moment you can finally see what's working.

That's why I reference B10 throughout this book. Not because I'm trying to make you memorize a framework, and not because I'm trying to lock you into a tool. Tools change. Pricing changes. Platforms change. The internet changes every time you get comfortable. B10, for me, became the simplest way to describe the backbone of a connected marketing system. It's not magic. It's not hype. It's not a funnel temple with seventeen pages and six secret upsells. It's just a sequence that protects follow-through so your business can be consistent without you having to become a machine.

When I say "connected," I'm talking about a chain of custody for your leads. I'm talking about the moment someone reaches out, and instead of that moment being held together by your memory and your mood and your availability, it lands somewhere reliable. It gets captured cleanly. It gets tracked in a way you can see then and down the road for visibility and tracking. It gets followed up on in a way that feels professional and human. And when life gets busy—as it always does—your business doesn't collapse because you missed one message at the wrong time.

The sequence I build around has a simple sequence when you lay it out: someone raises their hand, you capture it, you store the context, you follow up, you nurture the relationship, you communicate in a way that respects consent, you track what happened, and you improve the parts that leak, and you scale it for growth. You don't have to do all of it at once, you can phase it in and leave parts out to your preference. You don't have to do set it up perfectly, but you do have to understand the path, because once you see the path, you start noticing where your business is losing trust and opportunity without you even realizing it. From the B10, there are so many other marketing opportunities you can add and implement, but this gives you a throughline you can explore on their own, or all together.

It usually starts with the front door. Most businesses don't have a "lead problem," they have an "entry point problem." People can reach you through two phone numbers, three email addresses, a Facebook message, an Instagram DM, a website form, a comment thread, and a "text me" button—and you think that means you're accessible. But what it really means is that your leads scatter into ten different places, and now your life becomes a scavenger hunt. A connected path doesn't make you less accessible. It makes you more reliable. It reduces the number of places people can start, so you don't spend your entire week trying to remember where the conversation began.

Then there's the part that sounds obvious until it costs you money: if the lead isn't captured somewhere consistent, it isn't real. If a lead lives only in your inbox or your DMs, it's not a system. It's a hope. And hope is not a strategy when you're running a business and trying to stay sane. Lead capture is simply the habit—and the structure—of making sure every serious inquiry gets stored somewhere that holds the context, so you can pick it up again without reconstructing the entire story from scattered threads.

That's where the concept of a CRM stops feeling like something only big businesses use and starts feeling like basic self-respect. People hear "CRM" and think complicated, but at it's core it's just a home for relationship context. One place where names, notes, tags, and status live so you can treat people like people without relying on your short-term memory to perform miracles. It can be lightweight. It can start simple. The point isn't the tool, it's the visibility. If you can't look at your leads and answer, quickly, who needs follow-up and what the next step is, your business is running on recall instead of clarity.

And once leads are captured and visible, follow-up becomes calmer. Email becomes less about blasting and more about continuity—confirmations, next steps, expectations, reminders, and helpful information that keeps people from wondering if they fell into a black hole. When email is done right, it doesn't feel like marketing. It feels like professionalism. It feels like someone being taken care of. It's the receipt and the roadmap, and it's one of the easiest ways to build trust without being invasive.

But most people aren't ready on day one, and that's where nurture matters. This is the part small business owners take personally if they don't name it. Someone asks a question and then disappears. Someone follows for months and finally reaches out and then goes quiet. Someone says they love your work, but they don't buy. That isn't always rejection. It's often timing. Nurture is what keeps your pipeline from being all or nothing. It's the gentle structure that allows you to stay present without being pushy, so people who need more time don't fall off the map just because life got busy for them too.

Text messaging is where things get real fast, because it works and it can also go wrong. Texting is intimate, and that's why it requires more care. When SMS is consent-based and used respectfully, it reduces missed appointments, reduces back-and-forth, and makes people feel taken care of. When it's used wrong, it feels like somebody climbing through your window. So if texting is part of your system, it has to be treated like a privilege, not a loophole.

Then comes the part that feels intimidating until you realize it doesn't have to be complicated: visibility. Analytics. ROI. Truth. Most small business owners can't tell what's working because the trail is broken. They don't know where leads come from, what converts, what content actually creates inquiries, or what follow-up timing works best—so they guess. And guessing is expensive. You don't need fancy reports to get grounded. You need a way to track a few steady things consistently: where the lead came from, what happened next, what they chose, and what it produced. When you can see that, you stop marketing blindly, and you stop wasting money trying to buy confidence.

This is where optimization stops being a buzzword and becomes a relief. You don't automate everything. You automate trust breaks. You build a few small workflows where the ball tends to get dropped—confirmation after inquiry, a gentle follow-up if there's no response, reminders before an appointment, a simple check-in after delivery. These aren't fancy. They're just the quiet supports that prevent you from living in preventable messes behind the scenes. That's what I mean when I say automation can be a form of integrity. It keeps your promises without requiring you to remember everything at exactly the right time.

And scalability isn't bigger. It's cleaner. It's the ability to grow without everything becoming fragile. It's having a system that can be repeated and taught, so if you ever want help—or need help—your business isn't dependent on your memory and your availability for survival. A scalable system is one you can breathe inside. It doesn't demand heroics. It doesn't demand perfection. It carries the weight with you.

Let me make this concrete without turning it into a tech tutorial. Someone fills out your inquiry form. Instead of that message sitting there waiting for you to remember it, they receive a quick confirmation that tells them what happens next. You receive a notification that includes enough context to respond without hunting. Their information is captured in your lead list—whatever you use—and tagged with where they came from so you don't have to guess later. Their status sits in a simple stage like "New Inquiry." When you follow up, you're not rebuilding the story from scratch. If they book, expectations are clear. If they don't respond, there's one gentle follow-up so you're not staring at your phone wondering if you should circle back. And later, you can look back and know: where they came from, what they chose, and what it produced. That's a connected system. Not fancy. Not overwhelming. Just steady.

If you're building this yourself—and most small business owners are—you don't need a perfect tool stack. You need a preferred path that works reliably. That's why I'm also building DIY blueprints and guides that follow this sequence, because small business owners deserve options that don't require reinventing the wheel. But I want to be careful how I say that, because I'm not interested in locking you into a platform or selling you a promise that expires the next time the internet changes it's mind. The book is the principles and the path. The tools can be chosen based on your budget, your capacity, and your season.

And this is where the chapter lands: connection doesn't just increase sales. It protects your energy. It lowers the emotional toll of marketing. It keeps you from turning every inquiry into an emergency. It helps you respond consistently without living in your phone. And it gives you something most small business owners don't have—visibility. Because once you can see what's happening, you can fix what's broken, improve what's working, and stop spending your time and money on noise. Finally getting to reveal the ROI of marketing that you haven't previously been able to see with all the pre-B10 disconnected efforts.

But there's a reason the next chapter has to be about the cost of disconnection. Because the cost isn't just missed leads. It's missed peace. It's missed clarity. It's missed momentum. It's the slow drip of opportunity leaking out through cracks you didn't even know were there. So in the next chapter—"The Cost of Disconnection"—we're going to name it. Not to shame you. To free you. Because once you can see the cost clearly, it becomes easier to commit to the path that actually fixes it.

CHAPTER 8
The Cost of Disconnection

Have you ever woken up, pulled the covers back over your head, and thought, "Ugh, I don't want to do this today? Why does it feel like my business is running me more than I'm running it?" That moment is one most small business owners don't talk about out loud, but nevertheless is tends to cross our minds from time to time.

It doesn't usually happen all at once. It happens in small, quiet ways. You feel it when you wake up already behind, when you open your phone and see messages you forgot to answer, when you hesitate before checking email because you know there's something in there you've been avoiding, when you sit down to work and don't know where to start because everything feels urgent and unfinished at the same time.

And then there's this version of disconnection that doesn't get enough attention: losing access. Not the normal kind, like "I forgot my password and reset it." I'm talking about the kind that makes your stomach drop because you realize the business you're building isn't actually in your hands.

It looks like this: your Facebook Page gets tied to someone else's profile. Your Instagram is managed by a vendor who disappears. Your domain is registered under a web designer's email. Your Google Business Profile is "owned" by a former employee. Your ad account is built inside someone else's Business Manager. Your website hosting is paid by a contractor, so when they stop paying, your site goes dark. Your email list lives in a platform you can't log into. Your reviews are sitting under a listing you can't verify.

Disconnection doesn't always look like failure. Sometimes it looks like activity. That's what makes it so tricky.

A disconnected business can look alive from the outside. There's a website. There are social posts. There are conversations happening. There might even be sales coming in. But underneath it, nothing is anchored. No clear path. No reliable handoff. No consistent follow-through. Just a lot of effort holding everything together.

And effort has a cost. At first, that cost feels manageable. You tell yourself it's temporary. Once things slow down, you'll organize it. Once you hire help, you'll clean it up. Once you get through this season, you'll fix the system. But seasons stack. Busy becomes normal. And suddenly you can't remember the last time you weren't juggling.

Are We Connected?

This is where the myth of "just hustle harder" starts to break people. I've worked with business owners who were capable, deeply invested, genuinely good at what they do—and still drowning. Not because they lacked discipline, but because the business had too many loose ends pulling on them at once. Marketing wasn't one thing. It was ten things. And none of them talked to each other.

That's the real cost of disconnection. It fractures your attention. You're not just doing the work anymore. You're remembering the work. You're tracking the work. You're reminding yourself about the work. You're worried about the work you might be forgetting. And that mental overhead is heavy in a way people don't understand until they're carrying it.

The brain wasn't designed to be a project management system. When marketing is disconnected, every small task feels heavier than it should. Posting isn't just posting. It's remembering what link to use. It's checking if the website is updated. It's wondering if the form still works. It's hoping the message lands somewhere useful. It's guessing whether anyone will respond. And then it's waiting.

Waiting is exhausting when you don't trust what's happening behind the scenes. This is where I want to pause and say something clearly, because business owners blame themselves here: if marketing feels draining, it's not because you're bad at it. It's because disconnection forces you to hold too many moving parts in your head at once. That's not a skill problem. That's a systems problem.

I saw this in a new way once I was far enough removed from my corporate role to reflect honestly. Inside a structured environment, there was containment. Leads went somewhere. Conversations were logged. Progress could be measured. If something wasn't working, you could see it. If something stalled, it showed up. There was friction sometimes, yes—but there was also visibility. And visibility creates calm.

When I stepped away from that world and into entrepreneurship, the absence of structure was louder than I expected. I didn't miss the meetings. I didn't miss the politics. I didn't miss the red tape. But I did miss knowing where things stood without having to reconstruct the entire story in my head.

That reconstruction is where small business owners burn out. You shouldn't have to replay the last three weeks just to remember who you followed up with. You shouldn't have to scroll through old messages to piece together context before responding. You shouldn't have to guess whether a lead went cold or just got busy. And you definitely shouldn't have to wonder if your marketing is "working" simply because you don't have a clean way to see what's happening.

Disconnection creates doubt—doubt about your strategy, your offer, your pricing, and eventually yourself. And doubt is dangerous, because it drives reactive decisions.

This is where the shiny-object cycle shows up. You start thinking maybe you need a new platform. A new look. A new message. A new tool. You convince yourself the reason everything feels heavy is because you haven't found the right solution yet. So you buy something else, sign up for another subscription, join another training, download another checklist. And now you're even more disconnected than you were before.

I've been there. I've paid for tools I barely used. I've logged into platforms with good intentions and then never touched them again because I didn't have time to set them up properly. I've followed advice that made sense in isolation but didn't fit my real life. And I've felt that quiet guilt of knowing I spent money on something that was supposed to help me—but somehow made things feel heavier instead.

That guilt keeps people stuck longer than they admit. Because once you've invested in something, it feels wasteful to walk away. So you keep trying to force it. You keep it in the back of your mind as an unfinished thing. And every unfinished thing drains energy.

This is why disconnection is so expensive. Not just financially, but emotionally. A disconnected system trains you to live in reaction mode. You respond when something pops up. You chase problems instead of preventing them. You handle things when they become urgent instead of when they're manageable. Over time, urgency becomes your normal.

But urgency is not a growth strategy. It's a stress response. And here's the part most marketing books don't acknowledge: when your nervous system is constantly activated, your decision-making changes. You become more impulsive. You become more avoidant. You swing between overdoing and shutting down. You make choices based on relief instead of alignment.

That's when marketing starts to feel personal. Silence feels like rejection. Slow weeks feel like failure. Missed leads feel like proof you're not good at this. You compare yourself to businesses that look more "together" online and assume you're behind. And slowly, without meaning to, you start disconnecting from your own confidence.

This is why I believe systems aren't just operational tools. They're emotional stabilizers. A connected system gives you something to lean on. It gives you a place to put things. It gives you visibility so you're not guessing. It gives you consistency so you're not reinventing the wheel every week. And most importantly, it gives you back a sense of agency.

Agency is what disappears first in a disconnected business. When everything feels reactive, you stop feeling like the decision-maker. You feel like the responder. The cleaner-upper. The one trying to keep up. That's not why people start businesses. They start businesses for freedom, creativity, impact, flexibility. Disconnection quietly erodes all of that.

This is where the B10 Core Automation Method™ started to take shape for me—not as a framework I planned to sell, but as a response to what I kept watching happen to real people. People who were good at what they did. People who cared. People who were trying. People who were tired. I didn't start with "how do I automate marketing?" I started with "what's causing the most unnecessary stress?"

The answer was almost always the same: things falling through the cracks. Missed follow-ups. Forgotten conversations. Inconsistent responses. Leads landing in too many places. Data living in silos. Tools that didn't talk to each other. And business owners blaming themselves for what was really a structural failure.

Once you see that pattern, you can't unsee it. And customers feel it too. They notice when responses are slow. They notice when they have to repeat themselves. They notice when they're not sure what to do next. They may not say anything, but uncertainty is enough for people to move on.

That doesn't mean you have to be perfect. It means you have to be predictable. Predictability builds trust. And predictability comes from systems.

So we're spending time here—on disconnection—before we talk about solutions. Because if you don't understand the cost, you'll keep underestimating the value of building something connected. You'll keep thinking systems are "nice to have" instead of essential. You'll keep trying to push through pain that could actually be relieved.

As we move forward, you're going to see how each part of the B10 method addresses a specific type of disconnection—not all at once, not in a complicated way, but step by step, in the order that makes sense for small business. Because connection isn't about doing everything. It's about doing the right things in the right sequence. And when that sequence is right, marketing stops feeling like a constant drain. It starts feeling like support. That's the shift we're building toward.

Connection is the difference between effort that drains you and effort that compounds. Next: "Where Attention Lands".

CHAPTER 9

Where Attention Lands

Every business has a moment that makes the mark—the moment where Pay Now gets clicked and your bell for the register gets rung. Woohoo! You Got Paid. But what doesn't always make the mark are the decisions that happened just before the purchase. The micro decisions that happened and you probably didn't even notice.

They're the moments someone decides whether to take time to notice, click, message, fill something out, save your post, come back later… or quietly move on. Those are the moments that build trust and where attention lands. And for most small businesses, it's where everything starts to unravel.

We spend a lot of time talking about how to get attention, but almost no time talking about what happens when we have it. We focus on reach, impressions, likes, followers, views—the visible signals that make it feel like something is working. But attention is fragile. It doesn't linger. It doesn't wait for you to get organized. It shows up briefly, and then it decides whether it feels easy enough to stay.

If you've ever thought, "People are seeing me, but they're not converting," this is usually why. Because attention doesn't convert on inspiration alone. It converts on clarity.

I didn't understand this fully until I watched it fail in real time—again and again—across businesses that were doing everything "right." They were active. They were visible. They were even trusted. But when someone was ready to take the next step, there was friction. Confusion. Delay. Uncertainty. And uncertainty is enough to stop momentum cold.

This is where marketing stops being about creativity and starts being about infrastructure. In a connected system, attention lands somewhere on purpose. There is a clear destination and a clear next step. In a disconnected system, attention lands wherever it happens to fall—an inbox, a DM, a comment, a text message, or a contact form that may or may not still be working.

And when attention lands randomly, follow-through becomes random too.

Most small business owners don't realize how many places they've accidentally created for attention to land. A website form here. A "DM me" caption there. A link in bio that changes weekly. A phone number on Google. An email address buried on the contact page. Facebook messages.

Instagram messages. Maybe a booking link. Maybe a QR code someone printed months ago. None of these are wrong on their own. The problem is they're rarely connected. I know because I did it. Mitt on ready to catch whoever from wherever, however.

So attention shows up… and then it scatters. And maybe for a while it works, if you're the only one catching and throwing to the right bases, but it's exhausting to be the only place things can land. That's one reason marketing starts to feel like it follows small business owners everywhere. It's not just on a computer. It's in a pocket. It's at dinner. It's during practice. It's late at night when you finally have a moment to breathe—and remember there's something you didn't respond to.

That alertness feels like responsibility, but it's actually fragmentation. I remember the first time I felt the weight of this shift in my own work. I wasn't operating inside a system that routed interest to the right place. I was the router. And while that worked at first, it didn't scale with real life.

This is where business owners start living in a reactive posture. You check messages instead of managing flow. You respond when you happen to see something instead of knowing exactly where to look. You scroll back through threads trying to piece together context. You hope you didn't miss anything. And slowly, the business trains you to stay alert all the time.

That's not marketing. That's unmanaged attention. And unmanaged attention always turns into stress. And those reactions and related stress aren't healthy. And they're not sustainable or scalable for business.

Here's the truth that usually calms people down: most small business owners don't need more leads. They need fewer landing places. They need to decide—intentionally—where attention goes when it finds them.

This is where the first real "connection" in the B10 Core Automation Method™ begins. Not with automation. Not with campaigns. Not with content. With the capture. And containment.

Containment isn't flashy, but it's powerful. It means choosing one primary place where interest can land, QR codes can direct, socials can point to, and be leads can be captured cleanly. One system of record. One source of truth. One place where you can see what's happening without guessing.

In corporate environments, this is obvious. Leads go into a CRM usually by input from a sales team. Inquiries logged from their source. Follow-ups are assigned. It's not emotional—it's structural.

In small business, we skip it because it feels "too formal" or "too early" or "too complicated." We tell ourselves we'll set it up later, once things grow. But growth without containment doesn't feel like growth. It feels like chaos.

Containment is what turns attention into opportunity. Without it, even your best marketing leaks.

Think about how many times someone has said, "I meant to reach out but got distracted," or "I saw your post and then couldn't find it again," or "I wasn't sure how to contact you." Those aren't objections. They're breakdowns in the path. People don't need to be convinced to buy before they're ready. They need to be guided when they are.

That's why where attention lands matters so much. It's also why social media, by itself, can never be the system.

Social is powerful. It's expressive. It's relational. It's an amplifier and a fuel source. But it's original design wasn't intended to hold your business together. Although the future of social media is yet to be seen. It's designed to keep people scrolling. Messages get buried. Posts disappear. Algorithms change. Platforms shift. Social is the front porch. But you still need a house.

Your house is where attention is captured, acknowledged, and supported. It's where names, emails, phone numbers, and context live. It's where you can follow up without relying on memory. It's where your next step stays consistent even when you're busy.

When small business owners resist this, it's usually because they're afraid of becoming impersonal. They don't want funnels. They don't know how to "work" it. They don't want to feel salesy. They don't want to lose the relational part that made them start the business in the first place. I understand that fear.

But containment doesn't kill connection. It protects it.

A clear path is a kindness. It tells people what to do next without making them guess. It reduces friction. It reduces hesitation. It reduces the chance that a moment of interest disappears before it can turn into something real.

That's where forms, booking links, QR codes, and contact pages stop being "technical" and start being relational. A form isn't a barrier when it's done well—it's an invitation. A booking link isn't cold when it's clear—it's respectful. A QR code isn't impersonal when it leads somewhere meaningful—it's convenient.

The problem isn't the tools. It's the lack of intention behind them.

Over time, small businesses add things as they go. A form here. A link there. A page that seemed like a good idea at the time. Those decisions pile

Are We Connected?

up without a unifying structure, and suddenly nobody knows which path is the right one—not even the owner.

That's when the feeling of "I'm doing everything but nothing's working" starts to creep in. Because attention is showing up… but it doesn't know where to go.

Containment solves that. It creates one place where attention can land, be acknowledged, and move forward. It gives you visibility. It gives you context. It gives you back control. And control is what allows you to breathe.

One of the most underestimated benefits of containment is how calm it makes decision-making. When you know where leads live, you stop panicking about missing them. When you trust what happens after someone fills something out, you stop checking constantly. When you trust the path, you stop hovering.

That calm shows up in your messaging. It shows up in how you respond. It shows up in how confident you feel talking about your business. And people feel that difference.

So this chapter has one purpose: to help you see that attention isn't the end goal. It's the beginning. What you do with it determines whether marketing becomes a drain or a support system. And if you've been feeling tired, scattered, or behind, this might be the first place to make things easier—not louder, not bigger, just clearer. Because clarity is where connection starts.

Hold onto this: the work gets lighter when the path is clear and the pieces talk to each other. Next: "Why Lead Capture Fails".

CHAPTER 10
Why Lead Capture Fails

Most lead capture doesn't fail because people aren't interested. It fails because the moment doesn't feel safe enough to continue.

That's a hard thing to admit, especially when you've put real effort into your marketing. You've shown up. You've told the story. You've tried to make it easy to reach out. And yet the forms don't get filled out, the links don't get clicked, the inquiries don't turn into conversations—or they turn into conversations that go nowhere.

I've watched this happen in real businesses with real momentum. A client opened a new shop and needed branding and a grand-opening announcement. She also needed access to her website and social accounts—except a former employee still had the logins and never handed them over. Or maybe they did, but she couldn't find them. So, we built a workaround: a clean landing page and a simple email campaign that captured interest and routed responses into a CRM, so she could follow up later without losing momentum.

We planned to connect her point of sale to the CRM too, but the bulk of her customer contacts had been collected in notebooks for years. The time it would take to manually add years worth of data like that wasn't feasible within the timeline we had before grand opening. Despite a system ready, the result was still a grand opening, the good ole fashioned way. And it went off without a hitch. Nothing was lost even though we paused that part on purpose. She knew she needed a working digital foundation first to really make it all work, so the system sits, ready to connect once she stabilizes her cash flow and is ready to invest the time and money into rebuilding her foundation, with proper ownership and the connected system to help her save time, while optimizing workflows through connecting her POS database and her socials for the greatest visibility.

That situation is more common than people think, and it's also the clearest picture of why lead capture fails. It's not always the offer. It's not always the price. It's not always the message. A lot of times, it's the handoff—the moment between "I'm interested" and "I'm engaging."

Lead capture gets treated like a technical step—a form, a button, a link, a box to check. But lead capture isn't a technical moment. It's a relational one. It's the moment someone moves from watching to engaging, and that moment is fragile.

Think about how many times you've been interested in something but didn't take the next step—not because you didn't care, but because something felt off. The form asked for too much. The language felt vague. You didn't know what would happen after you clicked submit. You weren't ready to be sold to. You just wanted to feel safe before you opened the door. Those moments aren't failures of motivation. They're moments of hesitation, and hesitation is where lead capture either works—or quietly collapses.

Most small business owners unintentionally design lead capture from their own urgency instead of the customer's readiness. They want the inquiry. They want the booking. They want the commitment. They're thinking, "If someone is interested, they should just fill it out." But customers are thinking, "What happens if I do?" What happens if I give my email? What happens if I share my phone number? What happens if I book this call? What happens if I don't respond right away? If those answers aren't clear—or don't feel safe—people pause. And pause is often enough to lose momentum.

This is where consent becomes the quiet hero of effective marketing. Consent isn't just a legal checkbox. It's emotional permission. It's the feeling that you're allowed to move at your own pace, that you're not stepping into a trap, that you won't be pressured, overwhelmed, or regret engaging. When lead capture is built with consent in mind, it feels supportive. When it's built with urgency in mind, it feels extractive.

One of the biggest mistakes I see is asking for too much, too early.

Long forms.

Too many required fields.

Questions that feel invasive before trust is established. Owners justify it by saying they "need the information," but what they're really doing is front-loading effort onto someone who hasn't decided if the relationship is worth it yet. That imbalance creates friction, and friction doesn't always look dramatic.

Sometimes it looks like a form that gets started but never submitted. Sometimes it looks like someone reading your page and leaving quietly. Sometimes it looks like people reaching out in DMs instead because that feels safer than committing through a form.

Those behaviors aren't random. They're signals. They're telling you where the trust threshold is. Low form completion doesn't always mean low interest. A lot of times, it means the form is asking for more trust than the moment can support. Trust is cumulative. It builds through consistency, clarity, and tone. Lead capture works best when it matches the level of trust already established—not when it tries to force the next step prematurely.

Another reason lead capture fails is inconsistency in follow-through, and this one is painful because it's rarely intentional. A person fills out the form. They take the risk. And then nothing happens. Or it happens too late. Or the response feels generic. Or the response doesn't match the tone of the brand they just engaged with. That gap does damage. Silence after engagement creates doubt. Delay creates doubt. Mismatch creates doubt. And doubt erodes trust faster than most businesses realize.

This is where systems and humanity have to work together. You can't build trust if your response time depends entirely on when you notice a notification. And you also can't build trust if your response feels automated and cold. Both extremes break the relationship. The goal isn't choosing "personal" or "automated." The goal is choosing intentional.

An intentional response acknowledges the person, sets expectations, and buys you time without disappearing. It tells them they're seen. It tells them what happens next. It tells them when they'll hear from you again. That kind of clarity is calming, and calm is what people need when they're deciding whether to move forward.

Lead capture also fails when it isn't connected to memory. If someone fills out a form and then has to repeat themselves in the next interaction, trust takes a hit. If someone books a call and you don't know what they booked it for, trust takes a hit. If someone asks a question and your response doesn't reflect their context, trust takes a hit. Memory matters, and memory is where disconnected systems quietly sabotage good intentions.

This is why a form by itself isn't enough. A booking link by itself isn't enough. An inbox by itself isn't enough. They need to connect to a place where information lives, can be referenced, and can inform future interactions. That's not about being fancy. It's about being respectful. Respect shows up when you remember.

And the truth is: the smaller you are, the more important it is to be intentional. Big companies can afford to be sloppy. Small businesses can't. Your reputation is closer to you. Your relationships are closer to you. Your margin for error is smaller. You don't need complexity. You need clarity.

A simple connected system that captures the right amount of information, responds consistently, and remembers context is more powerful than a complex setup nobody uses. This is why I always come back to this: lead capture isn't about collecting data. It's about creating continuity.

Continuity is what makes people feel like they're not starting over every time they interact with you. Continuity is what turns a stranger into a conversation, and a conversation into a relationship. And continuity doesn't happen by accident. It's designed.

So if lead capture isn't working, it's rarely because people don't care. It's usually because the moment asks for more trust than it gives back. When you design for trust first, everything else gets easier. And when lead capture becomes an invitation instead of a test, connection starts to flow.

Real momentum isn't loud. It's repeatable. Next: "What Happens After They Raise Their Hand".

CHAPTER 11
What Happens After They Raise Their Hand

There's a moment that carries more weight than a business might realize. It's often overlooked as it comes to the business as a future sale, a check box, a win, even sometimes a sure thing. It's the moment after someone raises their hand. They fill out the form, send the message, book the call, scan the code, finally decide, "Okay, I'm in." And then they wait. I would personally compare it to the wait after the waiter delivers fantastic customer service all through the meal, and then takes too long to bring you the check or return with your card so you can leave. That waiting period is where trust either deepens—or quietly dissolves. And then all the hype, and for what?

I learned this the hard way with a client whose business had more history than her new systems did. Years of customer names lived in an old POS system that she had never pulled. We rebranded her website, executed a successful teaser campaign revealing the new branding, location, renderings, the new site launch and ultimately the grand opening!

Day one, her rebranded website, in combination with her new CTA form "Stay in the Know" with exclusive updates including an invite to the Grand Opening, went live—and I woke up to 500 entries sitting in an email inbox. A good problem to have... until it wasn't. Because 500 leads isn't momentum if you can't follow up. The next day, I created a CRM account, built an automation to map the form fields into the CRM, and then did the part nobody talks about: I manually entered the day-one leads into a spreadsheet, tagged, and uploaded them. That was the lesson: capture without connection creates chaos.

Now I build campaigns backwards. Where does the lead go? What happens next? Who replies? What's the first message? What gets tracked? Because the goal isn't "get more leads." It's "get leads you can serve." Then get more leads.

Most businesses don't think of silence as a problem. They think of it as neutral—a delay, a timing issue, something that happens because life is busy. But silence is never neutral to the person who just took a step toward you. Silence communicates something, whether you intend it to or not. It can communicate disorganization. It can communicate disinterest. It can communicate overwhelm. It can communicate, "This might be harder than I thought." And sometimes it communicates enough uncertainty that people back away before you ever realize they were there.

This is one of the most painful disconnects in small business because it rarely comes from neglect. It comes from capacity. You're not ignoring people. You're juggling. You're delivering services. You're with customers. You're handling payroll. You're living real life. You're answering what you see when you see it. And in that swirl, a message gets missed. A form submission goes unnoticed. A follow-up slips a day too long. From the inside, it feels understandable. From the outside, it feels like a risk.

I've watched this moment play out hundreds of times in businesses that were talented, well-meaning, and genuinely invested in people. Someone reached out at exactly the wrong time. The response was delayed. And by the time the business circled back, the energy had shifted. The urgency was gone. The moment had passed. The owner felt frustrated. The potential customer felt unsure. And both walked away thinking, "That just didn't work." But what actually didn't work was the space in between.

This is where follow-up stops being a sales tactic and becomes a trust practice. Follow-up isn't about chasing people. It's about honoring the moment they chose to engage. When someone raises their hand, they're not just asking for information. They're testing a relationship. They're asking: Is this business responsive? Is it safe to engage here? Will I be taken seriously? Will this feel easy—or hard? The answer to those questions is rarely in your offer. It's in your response.

This is why follow-up is one of the most underappreciated forms of marketing. It doesn't show up publicly. It doesn't earn likes. But it earns trust faster than almost anything else. The challenge is that follow-up often relies on the most fragile part of a small business: the owner's memory. You intend to respond. You plan to follow up. You tell yourself you'll get to it later. But later becomes tomorrow, and tomorrow becomes next week, and then it feels awkward to respond at all. So you don't. And now that person is gone—not because they weren't interested, but because the moment didn't feel supported.

This is where so many business owners quietly lose confidence in their marketing. They start thinking leads aren't serious, or people are flaky, or no one follows through anymore. But often, people follow the tone that's set for them. If the business feels uncertain, people hesitate. If the business feels responsive, people lean in.

Responsiveness doesn't mean being available 24/7. It means being predictable. Predictability builds trust because it removes guesswork. When someone reaches out and immediately receives acknowledgment—something that says, I see you, here's what happens next—their nervous system relaxes. They're no longer wondering if their message went into a void. They know they're in motion. That doesn't require a full conversation. It requires clarity.

This is where intentional follow-up systems change everything. Not because they replace you—because they support you. An acknowledgment message isn't cold when it's written with care. A confirmation email isn't robotic when it sets expectations clearly. A short note that says, "Thanks for reaching out—here's what to expect and when I'll follow up personally," does more for trust than a long, delayed response ever could. This is the difference between automation that feels human and automation that feels hollow.

When follow-up is built intentionally, it doesn't rush people. It reassures them. And reassurance is what keeps momentum alive. I've seen businesses transform simply by tightening this one gap. Nothing else changed. The offer stayed the same. The pricing stayed the same. The visibility stayed the same. The only difference was what happened immediately after someone reached out. Response times shortened. Expectations were clearer. The experience felt safer. And suddenly, leads felt warmer—not because they were different people, but because the relationship was being held.

Here's the shift that changes everything: being personal doesn't mean being manual. Personal means thoughtful. Manual means precarious. Manual follow-up depends on circumstances. It happens when you remember. It happens when you're not overwhelmed. It happens when nothing urgent interrupts you. That isn't personal. That's fragile. And when follow-up is fragile, trust becomes fragile.

This is why I believe systems are acts of respect. A system that acknowledges someone quickly is respect for their time. A system that remembers context is respect for their effort. A system that follows through consistently is respect for the relationship. None of that removes your humanity. It reinforces it.

One of the most subtle shifts that happens when follow-up becomes intentional is that you stop living in apology. You stop opening conversations with "Sorry for the delay." You stop feeling embarrassed about missed messages. You stop carrying guilt about things you didn't get to. That emotional relief matters more than people realize. Because when you're not weighed down by guilt, you show up differently. You're more confident. More present. Less reactive. And that confidence shows up in your marketing, your conversations, and your decisions.

Follow-up systems also create space for discernment. Not every lead is a good fit. Not every inquiry should turn into a sale. But when everything is manual, it's hard to tell the difference between someone who isn't aligned and someone who just needed a little more time or clarity. A connected follow-up path lets you see patterns. It turns what used to feel like rejection into information. And information is empowering.

This is where the B10 Core Automation Method™ starts to feel less like "marketing" and more like operational sanity. You're not automating conversations. You're automating consistency. You're not removing yourself. You're protecting your presence. You're not pushing people. You're guiding them.

And yes—there's a fear under all of this: what if I follow up correctly and they still say no? But clarity, even when it leads to a no, is healthier than ambiguity. A clear no gives you closure. A clear yes gives you momentum. Silence gives you nothing but stories. And stories are where confidence erodes.

This is why the space after someone raises their hand is sacred. It's not just a step in a funnel. It's a moment of trust. And trust is either reinforced—or broken—by what happens next.

As we move forward, we'll start looking at how follow-up evolves into nurture—how relationships are maintained over time without feeling forced or transactional. But before we do that, I want you to notice something: if your marketing has felt heavy, inconsistent, or emotionally draining, it may not be because you're doing too little. It may be because the most important moments aren't being supported.

When those moments are held well, everything downstream gets easier.

Marketing becomes calmer.

Decisions become clearer.

Energy becomes more stable.

And growth stops feeling like something you have to chase.

And starts feeling like something you're ready to receive.

Your next level isn't another platform—it's a cleaner flow. Next: "The Power of Staying Connected".

CHAPTER 12

The Power of Staying Connected

This is the sentence that can sting at first: if the power of staying connected feels heavy, something is probably disconnected—not because you're failing, but because the system is.

Most people don't buy the first time they notice you. They watch, listen, and observe how you show up. And then—sometimes weeks or months later—they decide.

That's one of the hardest truths for small business owners to accept, especially in a culture that worships instant results. We're trained to measure success by speed: how fast did the post convert, how quickly did the lead book, how many sales came in today. And when things don't move quickly, it's easy to assume something is wrong.

But buying decisions rarely follow a straight line.

People don't just decide based on what you offer; they decide based on how it feels to be near you over time. They're watching how you respond, noticing whether you're consistent, paying attention to whether your presence feels steady or sporadic. And even if they never comment or DM, they're forming impressions.

That's where nurture comes in—and why it's so misunderstood. Nurture isn't persuasion. It's presence. It's the ongoing conversation you're having with people who aren't ready yet, the quiet reassurance that you're still here, still doing the work, still trustworthy. It's what keeps the door open without pushing anyone through it. And I'll be honest: in my sailboat season, I didn't always have the patience for that. I wanted proof. I wanted traction. I wanted something that told me I wasn't wasting time. I'd post, check, refresh, overthink, and then feel that sinking disappointment when nothing happened fast enough to feel like it worked.

What I didn't see at the time was the invisible audience—the people who were paying attention quietly. I've watched businesses assume silence meant disinterest, only to hear later, "I've been watching you for a while." That sentence hits different when you've been questioning yourself, because what it really means is your consistency did something. It just didn't show up on the timeline you wanted.

This is where disconnected marketing quietly fails people. When communication stops after the first interaction, the relationship doesn't end dramatically—it just fades. The business disappears from memory.

The trust never fully forms.

Are We Connected?

And when readiness finally arrives, the person doesn't think of you; they think of whoever stayed present. Presence doesn't require constant communication. It requires intentional communication.

That distinction matters, because nurture isn't flooding inboxes or posting every day. It's showing up in a way that feels predictable and respectful. It's letting people know you're still there without demanding anything from them.

That's why frequency matters less than consistency. A business that shows up once a week in a calm, thoughtful way builds more trust than one that shows up daily and then disappears for a month. Inconsistency creates uncertainty. Consistency creates familiarity. Familiarity creates comfort. And comfort is what allows people to say yes when they're ready.

One of the most freeing realizations I had while building systems was this: not every interaction needs to convert immediately. Some interactions are seeds. Some are reminders. Some are reassurance. Some are simply a quiet touchpoint that says, "You're still welcome here." When marketing is disconnected, those moments get lost. Communication only happens when something is being sold, and silence fills the gaps. Over time, the relationship starts feeling transactional—even if the business owner has a good heart.

But when marketing is connected, nurture becomes part of the rhythm. It gets built into the system. It doesn't rely on inspiration or spare time. It doesn't disappear when you're busy. It's there quietly, doing it's job in the background. This is where automation, used thoughtfully, becomes a gift—not because it replaces human connection, but because it supports it. A simple check-in email, a helpful resource at the right time, a reminder of what you do and who you serve—these things don't feel pushy when they're relevant. They feel considerate. And consideration is what people remember

I've seen businesses change their growth trajectory simply by staying connected longer. They stopped assuming non-buyers were lost causes. They stopped taking silence personally. They built systems that honored the fact that people move at different speeds. And when those people were ready, the business was still there. That's the power of nurture. It shifts your mindset from "How do I close?" to "How do I serve until they're ready?" And that shift changes how marketing feels. It becomes less about pressure and more about alignment.

It also forces us to confront our impatience. We want things to work quickly because we need them to. We have bills to pay. We have goals. We have pressure—sometimes visible, sometimes private. Waiting can feel like failure. But patience, when paired with consistency, isn't passive. It's strategic. Strategic patience is choosing to stay present without forcing outcomes. It's building something that compounds quietly instead of chasing short-term wins that burn you out.

This is where B10 starts to feel less like a marketing system and more like a support structure. It acknowledges that relationships take time and builds for that reality instead of fighting it. You don't need to convince everyone. You need to be clear for the right ones. And clarity shows up over time.

One of the most overlooked benefits of nurture is what it does for you. When you know there's a system in place to stay connected, you stop feeling like every post has to perform. You stop attaching your worth to immediate results.

You stop riding the emotional rollercoaster of "good weeks" and "bad weeks." You trust the process because you can feel it working beneath the surface.

That trust changes how you show up.

You speak more confidently.

You make decisions more calmly.

You stop overcorrecting.

And people feel that steadiness.

Steadiness is attractive.

It signals maturity, reliability, and confidence—and those qualities matter far more than hype.

This is why nurture isn't a bonus layer. It's a core part of connection. Without it, marketing becomes a series of disconnected pushes. With it, marketing becomes a conversation that unfolds naturally over time. So here's the question I want you to sit with: if someone found you today and didn't buy, would they still feel connected to you a month from now?

If the answer is no, that's not a failure. It's an opportunity. Because staying connected doesn't require more effort—it requires better structure. And structure is what allows relationships to grow without draining you. That's the kind of growth that lasts.

Order creates peace. Peace creates follow-through. Next: "Seeing What's Actually Working".

CHAPTER 13
Seeing What's Actually Working

At some point, you've probably asked yourself, "Is this working?" It usually doesn't come out that cleanly. It shows up as second-guessing, as tweaking, as starting and stopping things before they've had time to mature, as comparing your progress to someone else's highlight reel. But underneath all of it is the same need—certainty. Not perfection. Not explosive growth. Just enough clarity to know you're not wasting your time.

This is where measurement enters the conversation, and this is also where it often goes sideways. Measurement has a reputation problem. For a lot of small business owners it feels intimidating, technical, and tied to judgment. Numbers feel like a scoreboard. Dashboards feel like homework. Metrics feel like something you're supposed to understand but quietly avoid.

And when measurement feels heavy, people usually swing to an extreme. They either obsess over it or ignore it completely. Neither one helps. What most small businesses actually need isn't more data. It's better visibility.

Visibility answers a different question. Not "How am I performing compared to others?" but "What's happening in my business right now?" That shift matters. Because when you can see what's happening, you stop making decisions based on anxiety and you start making decisions based on reality.

When I worked inside organizations with access to robust reporting, the most valuable thing wasn't the numbers themselves—it was the calm they created. We didn't have to guess. We didn't have to argue from opinions. We could see patterns, identify bottlenecks, and make decisions grounded in what was true instead of what was loud. That clarity changed how teams behaved. It reduced panic. It reduced reactive decision-making. It created alignment.

When I stepped into entrepreneurship, that clarity disappeared overnight. Suddenly everything felt subjective. Was this post better than the last one? Was this offer resonating? Was traffic up or down? Were leads ghosting—or were they just not ready yet? Without visibility, every decision felt risky. And risk creates stress.

This is where small business owners often measure the wrong things. They track what's easiest to see instead of what's most helpful—likes instead of leads, followers instead of conversations, reach instead of response. Those numbers feel reassuring in the moment, but they rarely answer the question that matters: Is this moving someone closer to a decision?

Visibility isn't about collecting every metric. It's about choosing the few that tell the truth about momentum. Momentum isn't flashy. It's subtle. It shows up in patterns over time, not spikes in a single week. It shows up in how many people move from awareness to engagement, from engagement to conversation, from conversation to trust.

And you can't see momentum if everything is disconnected.

When systems don't talk to each other, measurement becomes fragmented. Website data lives in one place. Forms live in another. Emails live somewhere else. Social engagement is scattered across platforms. Conversations happen in inboxes. Context gets lost. So even when you have data, you don't have insight.

Insight comes from connection.

Connection lets you follow the path. It lets you see where people enter, where they pause, where they drop off, and where they move forward. It turns numbers into narratives. And this is where measurement stops being scary and starts being supportive.

Supportive measurement doesn't judge. It informs. It tells you where to focus without shaming you for what didn't work. It helps you refine instead of overhaul. It gives you permission to stop doing things that aren't moving the needle.

And permission is powerful.

One of the biggest emotional drains in small business is feeling like you have to do everything "just in case" it works. You keep platforms alive because you're not sure which one matters. You keep offers on the table because you're not sure which one resonates. You keep tweaking because you're not sure what's landing. That uncertainty is exhausting.

Visibility gives you permission to simplify.

When you can see that most of your leads come from one or two sources, you stop spreading yourself thin. When you can see that certain follow-ups lead to conversations and others don't, you adjust. When you can see that timing matters more than frequency, you breathe.

This is why I believe measurement should reduce anxiety, not increase it. If your reporting makes you feel worse about your business, something is wrong with the way it's set up—not with you. Good measurement feels grounding. It anchors you in reality. It replaces stories with signals. It turns fear into information. And information is actionable.

Seeing What's Actually Working

This is also where perfectionism likes to sneak in. Business owners see data and assume it has to be optimized constantly. Every dip feels like a failure. Every plateau feels like a problem. But growth isn't linear. It ebbs and flows. It responds to seasons, capacity, and context. Measurement is meant to guide, not whip.

It's meant to answer questions like: Where are people getting stuck? What's being overlooked? What's quietly working that I should protect? Those answers don't require dozens of dashboards. They require alignment.

When your systems are connected, measurement gets simpler because the story is clearer. You're not piecing together fragments. You're following a thread.

This is where the B10 Core Automation Method™ quietly shines—not because it creates more reports, but because it creates fewer, better ones. It prioritizes visibility into the moments that matter: capture, follow-up, nurture, and decision. It focuses on what supports relationship-building, not vanity metrics. It respects the fact that small business owners need clarity, not complexity.

This kind of visibility builds confidence in a way that's hard to explain until you experience it. When you know what's working, you stop doubting yourself. You stop chasing every new idea. You stop feeling behind. You trust your process because you can see it. And that trust changes how you show up. You speak with more authority. You market with more ease. You make decisions faster. And people respond to that confidence.

Confidence doesn't come from having all the answers. It comes from having enough visibility to move forward without fear. That's when measurement becomes part of your support system instead of a source of pressure. It helps you protect what matters. It helps you refine without burning everything down. It helps you grow in a way that feels aligned instead of chaotic.

By the time you get to visibility, something shifts. Not because your business suddenly becomes perfect, but because you stop guessing. You stop treating marketing like a mood, or a gamble, or a performance that has to earn it's keep every single day. You start treating it like a connected path you can actually see. And once you can see it, you can stop spinning.

That's what B10 is trying to give you—not a pile of tactics, not a bunch of random "do this on Instagram" tips, but a method. A build order. A way to connect what matters so your effort isn't evaporating into noise. And if you've ever been stuck in that cycle—posting, tweaking, paying for tools, trying again, getting tired, pulling back—then you already know why this matters. You don't need more ideas. You need more visibility into what's working, and more structure underneath what you're already doing.

Because when you have clarity, you do less—but it lands harder. You stop chasing every platform. You stop overcorrecting. You stop changing your message every time the week feels slow. You protect what works. You refine what doesn't. You build with intention.

That's the promise of connection: it's not loud. It's steady.

But here's the part I can't pretend away. Most of us don't build this in a straight line. We learn it in real time—while we're tired, while we're busy, while we're trying to do the work and market the work and keep life together at the same time. We learn it through missed follow-ups, scattered logins, half-built systems, and the uneasy feeling that we're doing a lot… but still not sure if it's adding up.

Which is why the next section matters. Because the truth is, connection isn't just a strategy. It's something some of us had to learn the hard way.

Seeing What's Actually Working

PART II

Lessons Learned the Hard Way

My back pocket is weighing my pants down these days. The times I've said, "I'm so glad I have that person in my back pocket," are many. Over the last two years, I've met with AI experts in California, Denver, and the United Kingdom. Social media specialists in Argentina, New York, and California. UX/UI experts in Atlanta and Chicago. Automation experts in Florida and Canada. Successful mid-scale marketing agency CEOs in Portland. Sales experts from Illinois. Executive coaches in South Africa. Ghost writers and publishers in South Florida. Mentors I'm blessed to call friends abroad and in my own backyard.

The lessons I've learned are varying and vast. Some of them I've applied. Some of them I haven't been able to apply yet—not at the capacity necessary for impact, not consistently, not without the time or support I wish I had. But that doesn't make the lessons any less real. It just makes the season real. If you can use what I've learned to skip a few bruises, why wouldn't I share it?

I've wrestled with that line people love to quote—George Bernard Shaw, 1903: "Those who can, do; those who can't, teach." And I'll tell you where I've landed with it. I believe in what I've learned. I believe in the people who taught me. And I believe I have what it takes to bring it to life—fully. I'm still building. I'm still getting it tighter. But I'm not sharing from a pedestal. I'm sharing from the construction zone. And if you're reading this, chances are... you are too.

One executive coach took my call on the porch of his home in Africa. I had a hard time not looking past him—his background was full of tropical plants, and the peaceful scenery he had carefully curated for his escape was mesmerizing. He looked down at his notes, ready to deliver his assessment of my LinkedIn profile, and then paused like he'd decided to start somewhere else.

He began asking me what I was doing. Who I was trying to reach. How I help them. What my elevator pitch was. My offering. My value proposition. My competitive advantage. He leaned in closer and asked me my story—my why, my background. And then he stopped. Looked down at the paper with all the notes he had planned to go through... and said, "I like you. I trust you. I believe in you. Keep telling your story. I believe people need what you are bringing. That's it."

Then—almost like an afterthought—he rattled off the practical stuff anyway. Condense the headline. Comment with more than fifteen words on people's posts. Share your story two to five times a week so the algorithm can learn you and position you with the right people. Prioritize posting on your personal page, and share business announcements through your business page mainly for legitimacy, verification, and ads—because the engagement usually isn't there. The power is in trust and connections. Keep focusing on being you. Keep showing up candidly. Even LinkedIn favors that now.

And what I took from that call wasn't just a LinkedIn checklist. It was the reminder I needed in that season: when everything feels noisy, advice comes from every direction, and you're trying to grow while you're still carrying life… the thing that cuts through the chaos is connection. Story plus structure. Trust plus follow-through. The rest is just tactics.

So let's start with what it feels like when it finally clicks—when the pieces stop floating and start working together.

CHAPTER 14
When Everything Starts Working Together

One day, you wake up just like any other day. You make your bed. Brush your teeth. Get dressed. Fix your coffee and head to work. And realize that you forgot to fret. Something felt stronger about today. The business stopped feeling fragile. Not perfect. Not effortless. Just steadier.

In this moment, on this day, you realize you're not holding your breath every time you post, every time you send a follow-up, every time you wonder if the link in bio is actually doing anything, every time you open your inbox like it's a slot machine—hoping today is the day something finally clicks. You're still working. You're still making decisions. You're still adjusting. But the constant fear that one missed step could unravel everything begins to fade. The business feels less like it's balanced on your shoulders and more like it's standing on it's own.

And here's what surprised me the most: that moment doesn't come from doing more. It comes from things finally working together.

Up until now, we've talked about individual phases or parts that make up simplified marketing system following the B10 Core Automation Method™—attention, forms, capture, organization, follow-up, nurture, optimization workflows, scalable solutions, and visibility. Each one matters on it's own. Each one solves a specific problem. But none of them are meant to exist in isolation. Their real power shows up when they're connected.

This is the part most people miss. Most small business owners don't fail because they aren't trying. They fail because the trying is scattered. They're pouring energy into pieces that don't talk to each other—and when the results feel inconsistent, they assume the problem is effort. It rarely is. The problem is fragmentation.

Fragmentation is sneaky because it doesn't always look broken. Sometimes it looks like productivity. Sometimes it looks like "we're doing a lot." Sometimes it looks like a content calendar, a pretty website, an active Facebook page, a paid tool you don't even like, and a CRM you forget exists until you feel guilty again. Fragmentation often looks like movement, but the inside feels like translation.

And translation is exhausting.

You translate interest into action—because the person messaged you on Instagram, but your intake form lives somewhere else, and now you're trying to stitch together the conversation without sounding like you don't

Are We Connected?

know what's going on. You translate conversations into memory—because the "lead" is a name in one place, an email in another place, and a phone number in your notes app... if you remembered to put it there.

You translate data into decisions—because numbers exist, but they're not connected to the choices you're trying to make. You translate effort into hope—because you're doing the work, but you can't prove to yourself that it's building anything that lasts.

That constant translation is why small business owners feel tired even when things are "working." And if you've been that kind of tired—the kind that comes from carrying too many loose ends—you know the specific frustration I mean. It's not "I'm lazy" tired. It's "I'm doing everything and I still can't tell what matters" tired.

Integration removes the need for translation. When systems are connected, the story tells itself. Attention lands where it's supposed to. Information gets captured once and remembered. Follow-up happens predictably. Nurture continues without pressure. Visibility shows you what's moving and why. You're no longer stitching things together in your head—you're observing a flow that already exists.

And I need you to hear this clearly because it's one of the most freeing shifts in the whole book: the goal isn't to build a fancy business. The goal is to build a business you can keep. Not one that collapses the moment you get sick, or go quiet for a week, or have a family situation, or simply get tired of being the human glue stick, or the notorious dancing bear.

This is what your backend method was designed to do—not add complexity, not impress anyone, not turn your business into a machine—but create continuity, so the effort you're already making compounds instead of dissipates.

But here's where Part II gets real. Because the hard lessons aren't only about tools and flow. They're about ownership. They're about boundaries. They're about how easy it is to accidentally build your business inside someone else's ecosystem and not realize it until something breaks.

This is the part that doesn't feel sexy, but it changes everything.

At some point, most business owners have a moment where they realize they don't actually own what they thought they owned. Not because anyone is trying to steal it—most of the time it isn't malicious. It's just sloppy. It's rushed. It's "my cousin set it up." It's "my web guy did it." It's "my old employee made it with her email." It's "the agency ran the ads." It's "I don't remember the login but it's saved somewhere."

And then one day you're trying to log in and you can't. Or a contractor disappears. Or a password gets changed. Or your domain renewal fails because it's tied to a card you don't use anymore. Or your emails start landing in spam and you don't know why. Or your form stops working and the only reason you find out is because someone messages you on Facebook saying, "Hey... I tried to contact you and it wouldn't go through."

Those moments feel small, but they are not small. Because if your form is the door, you must test the door. And if your domain is not in your name, your business is renting it's address. That's not drama. That's digital reality.

That's why I started thinking about what I now call a control map—your digital deed. Not a spreadsheet to make you feel like an IT person. Just a simple, grown-up confirmation that the core assets of your business aren't floating around in other people's accounts like loose change. Because full control is rare. Full control is for ownership-level relationships. And ownership should come with a written scope and an offboarding plan—always.

That's a lesson I learned the hard way watching how "help" can quietly turn into dependency if you don't set it up right from the beginning.

And if you're thinking, "Okay Britt, but I'm small. I'm not a big company. I don't need all that..." let me gently push back. Even if you're solo, you're still the CEO of your business. And being the CEO doesn't mean being perfect. It means being intentional. It means you stop treating your business like a pile of apps and start treating it like a system with assets. It means you stop assuming and start verifying.

This is where the excess noise starts to show itself—not just online, but inside your operations. Because the internet will always try to hand you a new shiny thing: a new platform, a new funnel, a new hack, a new trend, a new reason to second-guess what you already built.

And most small business owners are already tired. Tired of posting with no traction. Tired of the algorithm changing. Tired of feeling like they're performing for strangers. So they reach for more. More content. More tools. More links. More offers. More "smart" automations they won't maintain. And then the system gets so complicated they can't keep it. Then it breaks. Then they feel like the failure.

But the system didn't fail because you failed. It failed because it wasn't designed for the way you actually live and work.

This is where integration becomes more than a strategy. It becomes emotional relief. Because when things are connected, you don't have to hold every detail in your head to keep your business moving. Your business stops requiring your constant translation. It stops requiring your constant proving. It starts supporting you back.

And that's the moment everything changes—not because you became louder, not because you became more "consistent" in the way people weaponize that word, but because you finally built something that could hold it's own weight.

That's the kind of robust I care about now. Not corporate-robust with departments and teams—just real-life robust. The kind that still works when your week gets messy. The kind that still works when you're human. The kind that still works when you're not in the mood to be a marketing influencer on a random Tuesday.

That's when everything starts working together. And that's when you finally get to exhale.

CHAPTER 15

The System Can Hold—But You Still Have to Lead

Okay, picture this. You finally get the pieces talking—and you expect relief. And yes, there's relief. But right after the system works, something else shows up: the system can't lead you.

The noise quiets.

The pressure eases.

The panic recedes.

The constant background hum that used to live in your chest—the one that told you something was slipping, something was missing, something was about to break—turns down so far you can finally hear yourself think. And instead of relief, you're left with a different feeling: responsibility.

Not the frantic kind.

The honest kind.

The kind that doesn't come with adrenaline. The kind that doesn't need an emergency to justify it. The kind that simply sits down beside you and says, "Okay.

Now what?" Because once the system can hold, there's nothing left to hide behind.

That's the part no one talks about.

When things are fragmented, you can always blame the chaos: the tools, the platforms, the timing, the learning curve. You can tell yourself you'll decide later, refine later, lead later—once things settle down.

Once the website is perfect.

Once you "get ahead." Once the content is consistent.

Once the next month is calmer.

Once you feel more confident.

But later becomes a habit when everything stays messy.

And if I'm being honest, the mess can be a strange kind of comfort—not because it feels good, but because it gives you something to point at when you don't want to look at the bigger truth. The bigger truth is that if the foundation is unstable, you can postpone leadership and call it survival.

But when the foundation is stable, leadership moves to the front.

That's what B10 was always meant to do. It wasn't designed to replace decision-making. It was designed to clear the runway so decisions matter again. It takes the weight of disconnection off your shoulders so you can actually see where you're going. It closes the loops that drain you. It quiets the parts of business that keep you stuck in reaction mode. And once you can see, you're responsible for where you steer. That's where systems end—and wisdom begins.

I used to think the goal was to get it all set up and then finally feel like I had arrived. Like stability would create certainty. Like a well-built backend would magically bring a sense of finality.

Like I'd wake up one morning and think, "Okay. Now I know what I'm doing." But what I found instead was space.

And space is beautiful… and terrifying.

Because space doesn't make decisions for you.

It doesn't tell you what your next move should be. It doesn't reward you for building a strong foundation by handing you a perfect roadmap. Space just makes the real questions louder—questions like: Who am I building this for?

What do I actually want this business to do in my life?

What kind of presence am I willing to maintain?

What am I not willing to trade for growth?

When the noise drops, the questions get clearer, and those questions don't have universal answers.

They have personal ones.

This is why I've always been careful not to present the B10—or even the 12.5—as something that replaces discernment.

They support it.

They protect it.

They give you room to practice it.

But they don't absolve you of it.

Because no system—no matter how well built—can make the hard calls for you. It can't decide what you say yes to. It can't decide what you walk away from.

It can't decide how visible you want to be. It can't decide how much of yourself you put into the brand. It can't decide whether your next season should be expansion or consolidation.

It can't decide whether the opportunity in front of you is aligned—or just flattering.

That's where the real work lives.

The B10 lives inside the 12.5 Marketing System™ for a reason. It's the engine underneath the story, the part that makes sure attention doesn't disappear, relationships don't drop, and effort doesn't evaporate. Social media, storytelling, brand presence—those things sit above it. They amplify. They humanize. They attract. But they don't steer. You do. And when you finally have a system that can hold, you start to realize something that can feel a little disorienting: your biggest challenges are no longer technical. They're human. They're emotional. They're strategic in a way that has nothing to do with tools.

You're not fighting broken links anymore. You're fighting your own avoidance, your own overcommitting, your own tendency to say yes because you can, your own fear of being misunderstood, your own discomfort with being seen, your own need to prove that you're legitimate by doing everything at once. And if you're reading this and thinking, "That's me," I want to say it plainly: you're not alone. This is the shift that happens to people who actually build something real. Because once you aren't drowning in chaos, you can't pretend the chaos is the reason you're stuck. That's when leadership gets personal.

I learned this the hard way.

Once my systems were connected, I realized the next layer wasn't about building more.

It was about choosing better.

I had to decide when to push and when to pause. I had to decide what kind of growth I actually wanted. I had to decide how visible I was willing to be—and at what cost.

I had to decide what I wanted to be known for, not just what I could sell. I had to decide what belonged inside my business—and what belonged outside it, protected, private, off the internet, not for public consumption.

And those decisions didn't come from a dashboard.

They came from experience.

They came from the moments you can't outsource.

The moment you realize you've been building in a way that impresses people… but drains you. The moment you recognize you're performing consistency instead of living it. The moment you feel the temptation to chase a trend because it looks like momentum—even though it doesn't fit what you're actually building. The moment you realize you've been making choices based on fear: fear of disappearing, fear of being forgotten, fear of missing out, fear of not being taken seriously. And once you can see those patterns, you're responsible for them.

This is where brand-building quietly diverges from marketing. Marketing is what you do. Brand is what people feel when they interact with you. And that feeling is shaped by thousands of small decisions you make over time—not just the polished decisions, but the messy ones, the tired ones, the ones you make on a random Tuesday when no one is clapping for you. How you show up when something doesn't work. How you communicate when you're unsure. How you respond under pressure. How you treat people when it's inconvenient. How consistent you are when no one is watching. Systems can support those moments, but they can't substitute for them.

This is also where integrity matters. When you're building a brand, your decisions compound in public. People don't just consume your content—they observe your consistency.

They notice when your message shifts. They feel when something is aligned or performative. They pick up on confidence, hesitation, clarity, and confusion.

And this is where a lot of business owners get stuck without realizing it: they think they need a better strategy, but what they really need is a cleaner internal yes and no.

Because clarity isn't just a marketing asset.

Clarity is a leadership posture.

Clarity is what keeps your brand from feeling scattered. Clarity is what lets people trust you without you having to over-explain yourself.

And clarity—real clarity—doesn't come from perfect planning. It comes from reflection, missteps, and course corrections. It comes from seasons where you realize you've outgrown something you once needed. It comes from moments where you recognize that a good opportunity isn't the right one. It comes from accepting that you can't build a lasting brand while constantly abandoning yourself to stay relevant. Those lessons aren't always clean. They're often uncomfortable. But they're what separate brands that feel grounded from ones that feel scattered.

This is where the builder matters more than the build. The B10 gives you a system that can hold growth. The 12.5 gives you a framework that scales visibility. But your brand is shaped by the choices you make inside those containers, and those choices deserve to be named. Because here's the truth: a system can hold, and you can still self-sabotage it. You can still overcommit. You can still chase too many directions. You can still dilute your message because you're afraid to choose. You can still make decisions that keep you busy—but not aligned. You can still build something that looks robust… and feels brittle.

That's why the next section of this book isn't about adding more structure. It's about naming the lessons that shaped how I use the structure—the things I wish I'd understood earlier, the assumptions that cost me time, the choices that made everything easier once I finally saw them clearly. These are not theories. They're not best practices. They're not commandments. They're the things you only learn by building it yourself: by watching what breaks, by noticing what drains you, by paying attention to what actually moves the needle—not just what looks good online.

In the next chapter—"Build It to Scale: SOPs, Vendors, and a Business That Doesn't Depend on You"—we'll build the next piece of connection so the system can carry more weight without you carrying it alone.

CHAPTER 16

Build It to Scale: SOPs, Vendors, and a Business That Doesn't Depend on You

The harsh reality is that the dancing bear theory is real. Once you're dancing, everyone throws money at you. If you, not a collective you, but you stop dancing, the money slows, even stops. If everything depends on you, growth becomes a trap. And a sneaky one at that. Because it looks like strength at first. You're capable. You're quick. You're the one who always figures it out. You can put out fires, smooth over hiccups, remember the details, and rescue the day with a late-night burst of effort that somehow makes everything work again—until it doesn't. And the shadow lurking around, peeking inside your door, planting seeds of exhaustion, yep... you guessed it, burnout, looms near waiting for the perfect opportunity to rear it's ugly head, rendering you spent. Checked out. So overwhelmed you don't even want to get up.

Because there's a point where "I can handle it" turns into "I have to handle it." And when your business only functions when you personally remember, personally follow up, personally fix things, and personally carry the load, you don't really have a business. You have a job with extra stress. And when you can't do another thing, that's when you really wish you would have built it differently to support your life, not drain it. This chapter is about the part nobody wants to do until they're forced to—not because it's fun or glamorous, but because it's the difference between a business that grows and a business that consumes you.

And if you're reading this as a small business owner who can't afford a big team yet, good. You can still build this. You just build it in stages, like you build everything else: one clean decision at a time.

There's a myth that keeps people stuck right here, and it sounds responsible on the surface: "I need a team before I can systemize." You don't. You need systems so that you can eventually have a team. The order matters. The right order is painfully simple and it's the part most people skip: you do the work, then you document the work, then you simplify the work, then you delegate the work, then you improve the work. Most people try to delegate before they document, and then they blame the team when it fails. But the truth is, the team can't follow what you haven't defined.

When someone says, "Just hire help," what they rarely tell you is that help doesn't magically create structure. Help actually exposes the lack of it. Because as long as you're the one doing everything, your brain is the system. You're the checklist. You're the reminder. You're the quality control.

You're the "I'll just handle it." And when you bring someone else into a business like that, they don't step into a clear role—they step into your head. The phrase too many cooks in the kitchen, yeah, let's just be honest, there isn't enough room for anyone else running around in your head but you.

That's where SOPs come in. An SOP is a Standard Operating Procedure, but don't let the term scare you into thinking it has to look like a corporate binder or a laminated manual. An SOP is simply "the way we do this here." It's the set of instructions that makes your work repeatable. It's what turns your effort into an asset.

SOPs create freedom in a way most people don't expect. They reduce decisions. They reduce mistakes. They reduce rework. They reduce the mental load of "how do I do this again?" And if you're a founder, that mental load is the hidden tax you've been paying for years. It's the reason you can be exhausted without doing anything "big." It's the tiny repeated remembering that drains you: where is that link, what did I do last time, what did I tell them, did I send that, did we test that, what's the order again?

SOPs are love in operational form. They protect your energy. They protect your team's clarity. They protect your customer's experience. They protect the version of you that doesn't want to be glued to your phone at 9:47 p.m. because you're trying to make sure nothing slips.

Now, here's the part where people get overwhelmed: they think they have to document everything. You don't. If you try to document your whole business at once, you'll quit. That's not a character flaw. That's reality. The way you actually get traction is by documenting what matters first—what happens often, what touches revenue, what touches trust, what touches the customer's experience, and what causes chaos when it's unclear.

That's where the core loops live. The core loops are the things that, when they're clean, make scaling possible. When they're messy, scaling becomes painful. They're the moments that create trust or break it. The moments where people fall through the cracks. The moments where you realize a lead came in and nobody answered. The moments where you're halfway through delivery and you're still deciding what "done" means. If you want a business that doesn't depend on you, start there.

And if you don't have the bandwidth to write out full SOPs yet, start even smaller: with checklists. A checklist is an SOP in it's simplest form. It's the shortcut that keeps your brain from having to reinvent the wheel every single time. It's the difference between "I think I did everything" and "I know I did everything." And that matters, because dropped balls destroy trust. Trust is revenue. Trust is referrals. Trust is the reason people come back. Trust is what turns a business into something stable.

Build It to Scale: SOPs, Vendors, and a Business That Doesn't Depend on You

Most businesses don't lose customers because the service was terrible. They lose customers because the experience felt inconsistent. Confusing. Unclear. Like nobody was really holding it.

This is why the format of your SOP matters. If it's too vague, it won't help anyone. If it's too long, nobody will read it. The SOP that actually gets used is the one someone can follow without needing you to translate it. It's the one that makes the task obvious, the sequence clear, and the finish line defined. If you don't want to write a whole SOP right now, write the finish line first—because "definition of done" is the secret to quality.

If you want consistent quality, you have to define what done means. Not in your head. In writing. In a way someone else can follow. Because a website page is not done just because it exists. A page is done when it works on mobile, when the form is tested, when tracking is installed, when links work, when speed is acceptable, when the client approved, when the customer can actually use it. Clarity creates consistency. Consistency creates trust. Trust creates scale.

Now let's talk about the other piece that makes or breaks scaling: people.

A lot of small businesses use vendors before employees. Freelancers. Agencies. Contractors. Fractional specialists. That can be smart. It can help you move faster. It can fill gaps while you're still growing. But vendors introduce a risk if you don't manage it with intention. If the vendor becomes the system, you lose control.

And people don't think that will happen to them until it does.

Usually it happens quietly.

The website is in someone else's account because it was easier. The domain is under the developer's email because they set it up. The social accounts are managed under someone else's login.

The ads are running from an account you don't own. The passwords live in a text message thread you can't find. The CRM was created by a contractor and now it's "their thing." It's fine… until it's not.

Until the contract ends.

Until the relationship shifts.

Until you need access and you can't get it. Until something breaks and the only person who knows how to fix it is gone.

This is why ownership matters. Even as a solo owner. Even before you have a team. Especially then. You own the foundation. Always. Vendors can build inside your system. They can support your structure. They can improve your processes. But they should not be your structure. They should not be the only ones who have the keys.

A clean access model looks like you keeping admin ownership, vendors getting role-based access, access being removed when the contract ends, passwords being managed securely, and a simple record of who has what. That's not paranoia. That's stewardship. If your business assets live under someone else's email, you're exposed. And you don't realize how exposed until you're locked out of something you assumed was yours.

Which brings me to one of the most underrated scaling tools that has nothing to do with marketing: a single source of truth.

Teams struggle when information is scattered across texts, DMs, email threads, random notes, and the unreliable phrase: "Didn't I tell you?" You need one home for SOPs, project updates, client status, and tasks. It doesn't have to be fancy. It can be a shared drive with organized folders and a clean doc. It can be a project management tool. The tool doesn't matter as much as the decision. Pick one. Use one. Commit. Connected businesses are organized on purpose.

And when you do that, you solve the problem that breaks most teams: handoffs.

Handoffs are where things fail. A lead comes in—who responds? A client books—who prepares? A project starts—who owns kickoff? A deliverable is created—who reviews? The work is completed—who closes the loop and requests the review? If you don't define handoffs, everyone assumes someone else is handling it. Then nobody handles it. Then the customer feels ignored, even if you did good work.

The fix is not complicated. It's leadership. It's naming the handoff in plain language: when X happens, Y person does Z within 24 hours. That's it. That's what makes a business feel held.

And here's the deeper reason this matters: scaling isn't just about adding more clients. It's about maintaining quality while you do it. It's about building a customer experience that stays consistent even when you're busy, even when you're tired, even when you're not the one personally touching every step.

That's what SOPs do. That's what clear ownership does. That's what clean handoffs do. They build a business that doesn't depend on you—not because you don't matter, but because you do. Because your job is not to be the glue stick forever. Your job is to be the leader who builds something stable enough to hold growth without breaking you in the process.

And if you've been carrying your business like it's a fragile thing that collapses the moment you stop paying attention, I want you to hear this

Build It to Scale: SOPs, Vendors, and a Business That Doesn't Depend on You

clearly: that doesn't mean you're doing it wrong. It means you're at the point where the business is asking you to level up from doing to designing. This is the part that turns effort into equity. This is the part that turns your knowledge into a repeatable asset. This is the part that lets you breathe.

Because when the operations are clear, growth stops feeling like chaos. And it starts feeling like something you can actually hold.

Next, we'll talk about the part no automation can replace: how you show up to lead what you've built.

CHAPTER 17
Social Media Reality

Here's the myth: social media is only for people who already have it "together." The truth is, it's often the thing you're using while you're trying to get together—while you're still building the backend, finding your rhythm, and figuring out what actually works for your business.

Social media can feel loud, while real marketing feels steady. And yes—social media can take you viral overnight. It can also take one awkward post, one misunderstood caption, or one off day and turn it into a public dragging if there isn't a system underneath you to catch what the attention creates.

I'm not saying that to be funny. I'm saying it because the emotional tax of social media is real, and most "best practices" don't acknowledge it. They talk like you have a full-time content team, unlimited energy, and a separate life that doesn't require you to be a human. Small and medium-sized businesses don't need more shame around social media. They need truth.

Truth is this: social media works best when it has a job. When it's treated like a role in a system, not the system itself. When you stop asking it to carry your whole business and start using it like the amplifier it was always meant to be. But before we even talk about strategy, we have to talk about the reality that trips people up—because it's not always creative. Sometimes it's technical. Sometimes it's permissions. Sometimes it's the difference between one harmless-looking button and another that will cost you time, money, and momentum.

Most business owners learn these things the hard way. They don't fail because they weren't talented. They fail because nobody told them what social media actually is. It's not one thing. It's layers. There's your profile and your posts—the part everyone sees. And then there's the part people don't see: business accounts, ad accounts, tracking, permissions, page roles, connected assets, logins tied to personal profiles, and a back-end structure that can either support your growth or quietly sabotage it. If you've ever had a Meta Business Suite headache, you already know what I mean.

Meta is the perfect example of why social media can feel so noisy. People think they're just posting. But the moment you want to do anything serious—schedule out, run ads, add a second admin, connect Instagram properly, set up tracking, manage messaging automation—you're suddenly introduced to a world where one wrong click or clicking too many things too fast can lock you out of your own business. And no one tells you that ahead of time.

I've watched this happen in real life. A business page that was created years ago, back when Meta's structure was different, gets passed around through helpers over time—same admin, but added an old employee back here, a vendor there, someone's personal account tied to it because that's how it was set up in the beginning.

Then one day the business owner, same admin the entire time, tries to do something simple like add a role, access finance settings, connect an ad account, or verify a payment method, and suddenly they can't—improper permissions. Not because the business isn't legitimate, but because ownership and permissions are tangled. And when ownership is tangled, support pathways for small businesses are thin, even with thousands of followers.

You can have a real business, real customers, real money on the line, and still feel like you're pleading with a system that doesn't care. You don't just lose time—you lose momentum.

You lose confidence.

You lose the willingness to even try again.

They tell you to run ads like it's a quick decision. But there's a difference between boosting and advertising that most small businesses don't understand until they've wasted money. Boosting is tempting because it's right there.

You post something, it gets some engagement, and Meta offers that little button like a candy bar at the checkout aisle: "Boost this post." Quick dopamine.

Quick reach.

It feels productive.

It feels like movement.

But boosting isn't strategy.

It's a shortcut.

It can be useful in a few situations, but it often gives you less control and less clarity. It's more like turning up the volume than building an intentional path.

It's visibility without structure.

Ads built intentionally through Ads Manager are different. They're designed for targeting, testing, objectives, and tracking. They're tied to assets, audiences, placements, and results you can actually measure. It's not just "show this to more people." It's "show this to the right people for a specific purpose." Most small business owners don't need to become ad experts, but they do need to understand that the button that feels easiest isn't always the one that supports growth. That's the pattern you'll see again and again in social media: ease and effectiveness are not always the same thing.

Another reality people don't talk about enough is permissions. Social media isn't just you and your phone anymore. If you have help—an assistant, a marketer, a contractor—you need structure, and the way you give access matters.

I've watched business owners hand over passwords because they didn't know any other way, and then end up locked out later. I've watched page roles get mismanaged. I've watched assets tied to the wrong account.

I've watched a business lose control of it's own presence because it wasn't set up cleanly from the start. And the worst part is none of this feels like marketing when you're dealing with it.

It feels like a crisis.

It feels like a distraction.

It feels like something you shouldn't have to know.

But if your business lives online, you do have to know it—at least enough to protect yourself. That's why I'm honest about social media reality. Because what costs small businesses isn't always lack of effort. It's lack of infrastructure.

Even something as simple as a collaboration post can go sideways if your accounts aren't set up correctly.

Collabs are powerful.

They're one of the easiest ways to expand reach without paying for ads, because you're borrowing trust and visibility through alignment. When a collaboration is done well, it doesn't feel transactional.

It feels like community.

It feels like endorsement.

It feels like shared value.

But collabs also require clarity.

Who is doing what?

Which audience are we serving?

What's the call to action?

Where does attention land?

Because if your collab post gets attention but your path isn't clean, you've just created a loud moment with nowhere for it to go. That's how businesses end up busy but not growing. They get attention, but they don't capture it.

They get engagement, but they don't guide it. They get visibility, but there's no next step that can hold the moment.

Carousels are another example of how social media rewards structure. Carousels work because they slow people down. They create progression. They invite swiping, which signals engagement. They let you tell a story in steps instead of yelling one message into the scroll. But the point of carousels isn't design. It's pacing. Small businesses often overcomplicate them. They turn them into mini brochures or cram too much in. The carousel doesn't need to carry everything. It needs to carry one thought clearly, with enough momentum that the person feels guided instead of lectured.

This is where social media becomes less about content and more about communication. Communication is your edge. You don't need to be the loudest brand. You need to be the clearest one. And on social media, clarity often wins because it's rare.

Now let's talk about one of the biggest traps for small business owners: thinking they need a different strategy for every platform. It's true that platforms behave differently. LinkedIn is built around professional identity, credibility, and story-driven thought leadership.

It rewards context and insight.

It doesn't punish longer form the way other platforms might.

TikTok is different.

TikTok is attention-first and pattern-based. It rewards hook, retention, and repetition. It can deliver reach fast, but it also requires comfort with volume and iteration.

Instagram sits somewhere in the middle. It's visual, relational, and community-driven. It rewards consistency, clarity, and connection.

It's where people often vet you before they commit. It's not always where they discover you, but it's where they decide if they trust you. Facebook still matters for local communities, events, groups, and older demographics with buying power.

It's not dead.

It's just different.

It's often more functional than trendy—especially for local businesses.

The truth is, you don't need a new personality for every platform. You need a consistent message and platform-specific packaging. That's where repurposing becomes less about copying and pasting and more about translation. A TikTok can become an Instagram Reel. A Reel can become a Facebook post. A post can become a LinkedIn reflection. But the tone has to match the room.

Repurposing is one of the most practical ways small businesses can show up consistently without becoming content factories, yet it only works well when your underlying message is clear. If your message is scattered, repurposing multiplies the chaos. This is why I always bring it back to the system. Social media is the fuel and amplifier, but if the engine underneath isn't connected, the fuel burns fast and leaves you exhausted with little to show for it.

That's also why link-in-bio tools can be both helpful and harmful. They're convenient. They give you one link that leads to many places. But many places is the problem. If you have five offers, three sign-up forms, two websites, a blog, and a random PDF link in your bio, you've just recreated the same fragmentation that makes marketing feel noisy. Your link in bio should not be a menu. It should be a path.

Most small businesses need one primary link destination that matches their current goal. That might be a booking page. A lead magnet. A product page. A contact form. A start-here page. But it needs to be intentional. It needs to reduce decision fatigue, not increase it. This is where clean URLs matter too. Small business owners underestimate how much trust is influenced by small details. A clean URL looks thoughtful. It looks stable. A messy link full of random characters looks risky, even if it's safe. People make decisions fast online. They don't always analyze. They feel. A clean path feels trustworthy.

This is also why messaging automation can be an asset when it's used with care. Automation can capture leads through DMs, deliver links, answer common questions, and create a smoother experience. But automation is never a substitute for relationship. It's a support for it. If someone messages you and gets something helpful immediately, that's a good experience. If they message you and get trapped in a confusing automated loop, that's a trust-killer. Automation should make things easier, not colder.

And that's really the core of social media reality: you're not just posting content. You're managing a front door. Front doors need to be welcoming. They need to be clear. They need to lead somewhere that can hold the moment. If your social media front door opens into chaos, people will leave quietly. If it opens into a clear, supported path, people will step in.

This is why I don't treat social media like an endless creative project. I treat it like a role. It's job is to attract attention, build familiarity, create trust, and guide the next step. When you treat it that way, social media becomes lighter. More purposeful. Less emotionally draining. You stop trying to win the internet. You start building a business.

And once you see what social media can—and can't—do for you, we can put AI back in it's proper place: support, not steering.

And when you build a business with a connected system underneath it, social media becomes what it was always meant to be: a powerful amplifier, not a pressure cooker.

CHAPTER 18

AI Is a Tool, Not a Decision-Maker

AI is first a tool. It can become a helpful, efficient, supporting "team member", but it is not inherently a decision-maker. The proper resources and deductive reasoning should be used before making important decisions.

While AI will happily help you build—but it will also happily help you stay busy. One of the most seductive things about AI is how willing it is to keep going. You can ask it to rewrite something ten times, twenty times, fifty times, and it never gets tired. It never says, "This is good enough." It never tells you to stop. It will happily keep refining, expanding, optimizing, and adjusting until you forget what the original goal even was. And if you're not careful, it will delete the original so much that it's almost unrecognizable. At first, that feels like magic. Then it quietly becomes a problem.

I've watched business owners fall into what I call the iteration spiral. They start with a clear intention—build a page, write a post, outline an offer—and somewhere along the way the work stops moving forward. Not because it's bad, but because it never feels finished. AI is always ready to make it "better," but better is subjective. And without boundaries, better becomes endless. This is where AI can either create efficiency or amplify indecision. The difference isn't the tool. It's how you use it.

Strong prompting isn't about clever wording. It's about direction. You have to know what you're asking for, not just what you're asking from it. That means giving context, constraints, and criteria—not handing over the steering wheel and hoping it takes you somewhere useful. Because AI doesn't know when your work is done. You do. Or at least, you should.

One of the most important lessons I learned using AI is that it reflects your clarity—or your lack of it. If your prompt is vague, the output will be scattered. If your prompt is overloaded, the output will be bloated. If your prompt has no stopping point, the output will keep expanding. This is why AI can feel overwhelming for people who already struggle with decision fatigue. It doesn't reduce the need for discernment; it increases it. That's not a flaw. It's a reality. AI is not a replacement for judgment. It's a multiplier for direction.

With many directions AI can take, this is why boundaries matter. You need to decide ahead where you want to go, how you think you want to get there, and have an idea of time you intend to spend, and what "done" looks like. Not perfect. Done. Live. Functional. Good enough to support the next step. That decision doesn't come from AI. It comes from you.

One of the most practical boundaries I set with AI is defining the role it plays before I start. Sometimes it's a brainstorming partner. Sometimes it's an editor. Sometimes it's a simplifier. Sometimes it's a second set of eyes that helps me see what I can't see because I've been staring at the same paragraph too long. But it is never the authority. The moment AI becomes the authority, momentum starts leaking. You begin deferring decisions instead of making them. You start trusting output over instinct. You start checking again instead of choosing. And confidence erodes quietly because you're practicing hesitation.

This matters more than people realize—especially for small business owners—because confidence is part of the brand whether you intend it to be or not. People can feel it when you're unsure. They can feel it when you keep pivoting your message. They can feel it when you keep revising in private but never ship anything into the real world. Shipping matters. Execution matters. AI should help you get there faster—not keep you circling.

This is where parameters come in. Parameters are not restrictions. They're guardrails. When you give AI parameters—word count, tone, audience, purpose, format—you're not limiting creativity. You're focusing it. You're telling the tool where the edges are so it doesn't sprawl. Without parameters, AI will fill every available space. With parameters, it becomes precise.

This is also where the emotional side of AI use matters more than people admit.

AI can feel validating.

It agrees with you.

It supports your ideas.

It mirrors your language.

That can be empowering, but it can also subtly reinforce overthinking if you keep approaching it like a judge. If you keep asking, "Is this right?" AI will keep answering. If you ask, "Is this aligned with my goal?" you get something more useful.

That's where Prompt Therapy™ lightly intersects—not as therapy, but as intentional interaction. How you talk to AI shapes how it responds. How you frame your questions shapes what you receive.

If you approach AI from uncertainty, it will give you more options. If you approach it from clarity, it will help you refine. Neither is wrong, but one moves you forward faster.

Another reality people don't talk about enough is that AI can be confidently wrong.

It can hallucinate.

It can misinterpret context.

It can give outdated or incomplete information. That doesn't mean it's untrustworthy.

It can say it's night when it's broad daylight.

It summary, it simply means it needs oversight.

AI should reduce your workload, not replace your verification process. A simple habit solves most of this: always ask, "What would I double-check if this were written by a human?" That one question keeps you grounded. It reminds you that AI is part of the process, not the final gatekeeper.

This matters even more when AI is used in public-facing work—websites, offers, legal-adjacent language, financial explanations—because confidence without accuracy can damage trust faster than silence.

So again, boundaries matter. AI works best when it has a clear role, clear inputs, clear constraints, and a clear stopping point. When you provide those, AI becomes incredibly effective. It speeds up drafting. It helps you think more clearly. It gives you options without overwhelming you. When you don't, it becomes noise. And noise is the opposite of AIfficiency™. AIfficiency™ isn't about using AI everywhere. It's about using it where it supports momentum, clarity, and execution for greater becoming.

Sometimes the most efficient move is to stop iterating and go live. I saw this firsthand with someone who decided he was done paying for promises. He'd worked with an SEO contractor for years and still felt like he couldn't tell what was real progress and what was just jargon.

So he turned to AI and started prompting it for SEO advice instead—page structure, keywords, headers, internal links, metadata, all of it.

At first, it felt empowering.

The suggestions were solid, and for the first time he could see the logic behind the recommendations. But every time he replied, AI came back with more—more optimizations, more next steps, more improvements that were technically true but practically endless. He didn't fall behind because he was lazy.

He got overwhelmed because he was trying to be the owner, the operator, the marketing department and now the SEO expert all at once. And that's the real lesson: sometimes the most strategic move is to do what makes the biggest impact, stop the spiral, and let the rest become a reach goal—or a task you hand to an expert when the business can support it.

You have to trust that what you've built is strong enough to learn from. You have to let the market respond instead of endlessly refining in private. You have to remember that real feedback comes from real interaction, not hypothetical improvement. AI can help you prepare. Only action helps you progress. If you keep that distinction clear, AI becomes one of the most powerful tools in your ecosystem. If you don't, it becomes another shiny thing that promises clarity while quietly delaying movement.

The choice isn't whether to use AI. The choice is whether you're leading it—or letting it lead you.

One of the easiest ways to tell when AI is starting to 'drive' instead of assist is when you feel yourself chasing perfect. You ask for a rewrite, then another rewrite, then another—until you've edited the soul out of what you meant. The tool didn't fail you. It did what tools do: it kept producing options. The decision belongs to you. The moment you define what 'done' looks like, the overwhelm drops because you stop outsourcing discernment.

Here's a guardrail that saved me: I decide the point of the piece before I ask for help. Not the whole outline, just the point. What is this supposed to accomplish? Who is it for? What should someone feel or do after reading it? How much of my voice do I want to maintain in the output? When you can answer those four questions, AI becomes an amplifier instead of a replacement. It helps you get there faster, but it can't tell you where 'there' is. That's leadership, not prompting.

Another guardrail is language ownership. If a sentence doesn't sound like you, you don't owe it loyalty just because it's 'good.' A lot of AI output sounds polished, but polish isn't always persuasion. Your voice carries lived experience, nuance, and truth. The goal is not to sound impressive. The goal is to sound clear, steady, and real. AI can help you refine that voice, but you still get the final vote.

This is also where people get tripped up by the idea of 'objectivity.' They assume AI can be neutral, and therefore better. But neutrality without context can become noise. Your business has context. Your audience has context. Your season has context. The more you can give that context—your values, your boundaries, the way you actually operate—the more useful the tool becomes. Without context, it will keep offering generic answers that feel like they belong to everyone and no one at the same time.

AI Is a Tool, Not a Decision-Maker

So if you're learning to use AI without letting it run you, start simple: decide what matters, ask for help with structure, and keep your discernment in your own hands. The tool can speed up motion, but only you can protect meaning. And that's the real win—using technology to support your building, not replace your leadership.

AI is most useful when you treat it like a mirror and a builder's assistant at the same time. Let it reflect what you're saying back to you so you can hear yourself, then let it help you tighten structure. But keep the meaning in your hands. Meaning is the part that builds trust, and trust is the part that sells.

Practically, this can look like setting a decision checkpoint. After two rounds of drafts, you stop and ask: is this clearer than my original, or just different? If it's just different, you keep your original and move forward. That one habit prevents the endless loop of 'almost there' edits that drain time and confidence.

From there, we have to talk about the next trap: selling across channels without letting the channels steal your peace.

CHAPTER 19

Selling Across Channels Without Losing Your Mind

Picture this: you have your offer, you've thought out your messaging, you decided your price, you even found some brand-forward template on Canva to help you get a post pulled together—price and all. And you post the link.

Inevitably, someone asks for the price anyway. Another person wants to pay a different way. Suddenly you're DM'ing, invoicing, and chasing details—on three different platforms. Selling looks simple from the outside.

I didn't understand this at first, because selling feels like the reward. You built something. You published it. You put it out into the world. Of course selling should be the easy part, right? Not exactly. Each platform has it's own rules, it's own economics, and it's own definition of what "integrated" actually means. And if you don't know what those definitions are, you can end up paying for convenience with confusion.

Amazon is a perfect example. Amazon is powerful because it already has traffic—that's the promise. You're stepping into a marketplace where people are already searching, already buying, already trusting the checkout process. That's incredibly valuable, especially for books and physical products. But that value comes with trade-offs. Amazon owns the customer relationship. Amazon controls the data you see. Amazon sets the fees. Amazon decides what is visible and what isn't. When you sell on Amazon, you're borrowing trust, but you're also borrowing space. And borrowed space always comes with conditions.

This is where many small business owners get tripped up with merch and bundles. You upload a shirt, a sweatshirt, a mug, or a book bundle, and everything looks fine on the surface. The product is live. The listing exists. Orders may even come in. But behind the scenes, something doesn't quite sit right. Your products show as "generic." Your brand isn't verified. Your storefront doesn't look like yours. And suddenly you realize there were steps you didn't know you had to take first.

That "generic" label hit me like a brick because it wasn't a design problem—it was a backend problem. I had book bundles, shirts, mugs—things I was proud to finally sell—and I didn't realize Amazon was quietly asking a different question: do you have permission to sell this brand, and can you prove what this product is? I learned the hard way that those GTINs (Global Trade Item Numbers—like UPCs/EANs) aren't a technical detail you can ignore. They're part of how Amazon decides what

Are We Connected?

your product is, who it belongs to, and whether you're building your catalog like a brand or like a random listing floating in the marketplace.

And the thing is—this isn't just an Amazon thing. Once you start paying attention, you realize GTINs are a whole language in the product world. They're part of what makes your products legible at scale, especially if you ever want to move beyond one-off sales and into bigger distribution conversations. A lot of large retail ecosystems and buying pipelines use third-party product discovery and intake platforms like RangeMe. That's where your identifiers matter long before anyone ever sees your product on a shelf. I didn't understand that early on—I thought barcodes were just for checkout. But they're also a signal: this is a real product, from a real brand, built in a way that can be tracked, verified, and carried.

And since I'm already being honest… I just learned how universal that is. QVC has routed product submissions through RangeMe. And I recently found out retailers like ACE and Lowe's use it too. I even bought a company prefix and GTINs today for the company I work for and registered products in premarket—because if you're aiming toward bigger distribution, you don't wait until the last minute to speak the language.

That's where exemptions come in. For certain products and categories, Amazon can allow you to list without buying external barcodes—if you apply the right way, in the right order, and your brand is set up to support it. And the catch is the order. If you list first and learn later, you may not get a clean "edit" option. Sometimes the only clean path forward is to rebuild the listing correctly from the start.

When you're selling bundles—like pairing a book with a mug, or a shirt with a workbook—the backend has to match the real world. Otherwise the system treats your offer like a mismatch, and you spend days, even weeks, trying to fix a problem that isn't on the product page at all. And once you build the catalog the wrong way, it can feel like there's no clean rewind button. You don't just "fix it later." You end up rebuilding listings, re-uploading products, and untangling decisions you didn't even know you were making—because nobody tells you the backend rules until you break one.

And it can be costly. The Seller Central fees don't stop while your products are hard to find. They keep on rolling for your rented space. And when you do make sales, there are more fees to find assessed.

That's not failure. That's tuition. And maybe intuition for you, but it was one of those moments where "selling across channels" stopped being theoretical and became very real for me. Each platform has a preferred order of operations, and they don't always explain it in a way that makes sense to someone who's building for the first time.

Shopify is different. Shopify gives you control. You own the storefront. You own the customer relationship. You control the branding, the checkout experience, the data, and the integrations. You manage the SKUs. But with that control comes responsibility. You pay subscription fees. You're responsible for traffic. You're responsible for setup. You're responsible for plugins, apps, and maintenance. Taxes. Shipping. Policies. Shopify doesn't bring customers to you; it gives you a place to send them. That's a critical distinction. If Amazon is a marketplace you step into, Shopify is land you build on. Neither is better in every situation. They serve different purposes.

TikTok Shop adds another layer entirely. TikTok Shop can create demand quickly, especially for physical products, because it blends content and commerce in real time. But it also introduces platform-specific fees, fulfillment expectations, and policies that change fast. It's momentum-based. That means if you're going to sell there, you need systems that can handle bursts—orders coming in faster than usual, inventory moving unexpectedly, questions piling up. If your backend isn't ready for that, visibility becomes stress instead of opportunity.

Here's the pattern across all selling channels: growth exposes gaps. Selling more doesn't fix a shaky system; it reveals it. That's why it's so important to understand the roles and the routes. "Integrated" doesn't mean connected in theory. It means connected in practice. It means when someone buys something, you know where the order came from, how it's fulfilled, how it's tracked, how the money moves, and how the customer is followed up with. If any of those pieces are unclear, selling starts to feel chaotic—even when sales are coming in.

This is the part most people don't say out loud: most of the stress in multi-channel selling isn't the selling. It's the tracking. It's remembering which version of your offer lives where, which link is current, which message thread has the most context, and which customer already paid. When that information is scattered, your brain becomes the bridge—and bridges break when they carry too much weight for too long.

The calmer approach is to choose a source of truth and let everything point back to it. That could be one checkout link, one form, one CRM pipeline, one booking page—whatever fits your business. The channel is just the front door. The system behind it is the house. When every channel routes to the same place, you stop feeling like you're selling in ten directions at once.

Another hidden stressor is policy inconsistency. When you sell across platforms, you need one consistent set of expectations: refund policy, delivery timeline, how you communicate, where support lives. If those details change depending on the platform, customers get confused and you get buried in messages. A simple, consistent policy page or confirmation email does more for your sanity than most people realize.

This is also where automation can be kind instead of cold. A quick confirmation, a clear next step, a simple "here's what to expect" message—that's not corporate. That's care. It reduces the back-and-forth. It prevents misunderstandings. And it lets you show up as a human without being on-call 24/7.

And if you're worried that automation makes you feel distant, remember: clarity is kindness. People don't need you to be available at all hours. They need to know what to do. When you give them that, you protect your energy and you protect their experience at the same time.

This is also where your ecosystem matters. Books behave differently than merch. Books are often the first point of trust. Merch is often an extension of identity. People buy books to understand. They buy merch to belong. When those things are connected—when the book leads somewhere and the merch reinforces the message—selling feels cohesive instead of scattered. It feels like a natural extension of the relationship, not a random offer thrown into the feed.

Selling across channels is not about domination. It's about alignment—alignment between product and platform, alignment between visibility and capacity, alignment between ambition and infrastructure. When those things line up, selling becomes sustainable. When they don't, even good sales can feel like a burden. I learned that the hard way—not because I wasn't capable, but because I was learning in motion, and that learning changed how I build now.

Now, I don't ask, "Where can I sell this?" I ask, "Where does this belong right now?" That one question simplifies everything. Because when you sell from connection instead of pressure, each channel supports the ecosystem instead of competing with it. And that's the difference between selling more and building something that lasts.

CHAPTER 20

Integrations, Fees, and the Truth About "Easy"

"Easy" is one of the most expensive words in business.

The first time I heard someone say, "Just sell it on Amazon," it was delivered with the same tone people use when they say, "Just throw it in the cart," like the hardest part was deciding to do it. Like Amazon was a lane you could casually merge into if you had a decent product and a little motivation. And I get why people say it that way. From the outside, it looks like the easiest thing in the world. Amazon already has traffic, Amazon already has buyers, Amazon already has the machine. You just bring your product and let the river carry you.

But once you step into it—once you actually create the account, list the product, start building the catalog, and look at what it takes to sell—you realize the truth. Amazon is not a lane. It's a toll road. And so are a lot of the platforms we're told will make selling "easy," because easy is rarely free. Easy is rarely simple. Easy is usually pre-built infrastructure that you're renting, and rent always comes with terms.

I learned that lesson the first time I looked something up once—one time—and then felt like the internet decided to adopt me. A pair of shoes. A countertop appliance. A random business tool I clicked on at midnight because a guru said it would "save hours." The next day, there it was again: Instagram, Facebook, YouTube, a banner ad on a news site. The next day, there it was again: Instagram, Facebook, YouTube, a banner ad on a news site. And honestly? It can feel creepy—like the internet listened to you. Sometimes it's not even that dramatic; it's just the combination of search history, app permissions, location data, and tracking—cookies, pixels, retargeting—quiet little breadcrumbs that tell platforms who you are and what you might buy next.

As a business owner, that's both powerful and unsettling. Powerful because it means you can stay in front of the right people after they visit your site. Unsettling because you realize how much of "easy marketing" is really rented visibility you only keep if you keep paying—either with money, with data, or with both.

And this is where integrations start to feel personal, because you don't just set up a pixel and walk away. You connect accounts, verify domains, accept policies, manage permissions, and then you wait to see if the machine is doing what you think it's doing. If you've ever felt behind because you didn't know what a pixel was, you're not behind—you're normal. A pixel is a small tracking code you get from an ad platform—Meta, Google,

Are We Connected?

TikTok—that you install on your website so the platform can recognize visitors and track actions (like view, click, add-to-cart, purchase). It's what makes retargeting possible. It's also what makes people feel like their phone is reading their mind. And the reason it gets personal is because it forces you to connect the behind-the-scenes dots: your site, your domain, your ad account, your permissions, your policies... all the stuff nobody mentions when they say "just run an ad."

Most small business owners weren't taught this. We were taught to work hard, not to become part-time internet engineers.

What I didn't understand early on is that the cost of selling online isn't just the cost of making the product. It's the cost of standing in the marketplace. It's the price of access. And most small business owners don't realize how many hands touch their money before it ever touches their account.

You can price something with confidence, feel proud of your offer, finally get a sale... and then open your dashboard and feel a quiet kind of insult when the payout doesn't match what your brain expected. Not because you were wrong. Because you were uninformed. Because nobody sits you down at the beginning and says, "Here's how the math actually works." They just say, "It's easy."

This is why I'm blunt about fees. Not because fees are evil. Fees are normal. Fees are the cost of infrastructure. The problem isn't the fees—it's the surprises. It's the way you can accidentally build your pricing, your expectations, and your business model on numbers that aren't real enough once the platform takes it's cut.

Amazon is the clearest example because it's the biggest machine, and it's the one people recommend the fastest. Seller Central looks official. It feels like you're graduating into real commerce. But even getting set up can feel like you're trying to enter a building where nobody put signs on the doors. You learn quickly that there are different account paths, different fees, different requirements, different categories with different rules, different fulfillment options that change your margins, different visibility systems that decide whether you're seen, and different, sometimes hard to wrangle customer service.

And then you learn the part that hits small businesses the hardest: the platform can be the customer, not your customer. Meaning, you don't actually own the relationship. You're renting the audience. You're renting the visibility. You're renting the trust people already have in the marketplace. And marketplaces don't rent you anything without taking their cut.

Integrations, Fees, and the Truth About "Easy"

Sometimes it's a clean percentage. Sometimes it's layers of fees stacked so quietly you don't notice until you compare what you made to what you received. That's where the truth about "easy" shows up. Easy means you don't have to build the road. But it also means you don't control the tolls.

I learned this not just through Amazon, but through the entire ecosystem of platforms we're told are "simple" for small businesses. Shopify looks straightforward until you realize your payment processor still takes a percentage, you may pay for apps to do what you assumed the store would do, and you're responsible for taxes, shipping settings, policies, and maintenance. TikTok Shop looks like a sales miracle until you realize you're dealing with platform rules, shipping expectations, refund patterns, and fee structures that aren't designed around your peace. Instagram makes it feel like you can go from post to profit, but then you discover that visibility is not guaranteed, and the add-ons that make it "work" have their own costs—whether it's boosting, advertising, or the tools you need to manage messages, link routing, and automation.

None of this is meant to scare you. It's meant to sober you. Because the real danger isn't the fees. The real danger is building your pricing and your expectations without understanding the fees.

This is where so many small business owners start feeling discouraged. They don't say it out loud because they think they're supposed to be grateful for the sale. But the math can feel like betrayal if you weren't prepared. You think you're making one number, and the platform quietly reminds you that you're actually making another.

I had to learn to stop pricing based on what I wanted to earn and start pricing based on what the system would take. That shift is not glamorous, but it's foundational. Because if you're selling a physical product, your costs aren't just materials. They're packaging. They're labels. They're shipping supplies. They're storage. They're time. They're replacements. They're customer service. They're returns. They're platform cuts. They're payment processing. They're the app that prints labels. They're the subscription that manages inventory. All of that comes out before profit becomes profit.

And it's not just the platform fees. It's the "little boxes" too—the settings you click when you're moving fast. I somehow enabled advertising for one of my published works for almost a year that I couldn't figure out where it was coming from. Even when I called, they couldn't find the account. The end date is a key factor on all advertising setups. If you don't set an end date, it will continue to run and automatically renew after a year. Of course policies do not allow for refunds, and something as little as a box you check—or don't uncheck—can make a big difference in your bottom line.

That is an innocent lesson learned the hard way. That's what happens when you're building in motion and nobody is teaching the backend reality while they're selling you the dream.

This is also why the word integration gets thrown around like it means simplicity. "Just integrate Shopify with Amazon." "Just integrate TikTok Shop." "Just sync your products." "Just connect your catalog." "Just link your payment processor." "Just connect your email marketing." There is nothing "just" about it. Because every integration adds another layer of terms, rules, settings, and points of failure.

Integrations can be powerful, but they're not magic. An integration might sync products but not inventory. It might sync inventory but not fulfillment. It might sync orders but not customer data. It might connect the front end while the back end still leaks. That's why the best way to stay sane is to stop treating integrations like a promise and start treating them like a bridge. Bridges need inspection.

Here's a simple practice that saves more stress than most "growth hacks" ever will: before you announce a new offer or move a checkout, run one clean test purchase. See what email arrives. See what information you get. See what the customer sees. Most tech headaches are really untested paths. A ten-minute test can save you hours of apologizing later.

And when something breaks—and it will—having one backup plan keeps you from spiraling. A manual invoice link. A simple form. A direct payment button. You're not building for a world where nothing fails. You're building for a world where you can recover quickly without losing your peace.

The moment I stopped resenting the fees and started understanding them, I got my power back. Because resentment kept me reactive, but understanding made me strategic. It made me ask better questions before I invested time in a platform. It made me look at profitability differently. It made me stop chasing what looked popular and start choosing what was sustainable.

So here's the truth I wish I had internalized sooner: if you don't know your platform fees, you don't know your profit. And if you don't know your profit, you don't actually know if your business is working. You might be getting sales and still losing ground. You might be building visibility and still starving your margin. You might be "busy" and still not safe.

And the truth about "easy" is this: easy is not about fewer steps. Easy is about fewer surprises. When you understand the toll roads, you stop getting blindsided. And when you stop getting blindsided, you can build something that lasts.

Because scaling a system that doesn't make money is not growth. It's acceleration into burnout.

CHAPTER 21

Products + Backend Protection

When money starts moving, admin gets louder. There's a moment in every small business where things start to multiply—offers, platforms, files, payments—and you realize the backend matters just as much as the front.

Most small business owners don't learn this until they get burned.

Not in theory, but in real, expensive ways.

Getting locked out of a Facebook Page. Discovering you don't actually own the domain you thought you paid someone to buy. Watching an Amazon listing get trapped under "generic" because the brand wasn't established first.

Realizing too late that a partner situation wasn't clarified. Learning a vendor still holds the keys to your accounts. Hitting a name conflict you didn't see coming.

None of those things are creative problems.

They're ownership problems.

They're protection problems.

They're the kind of problems you don't know you have until the day they cost you.

This was one of the most humbling lessons I learned, because on the surface everything looked fine. Products were created. Listings existed. Orders could come through. But underneath that surface was a layer I hadn't fully understood yet—identifiers, codes, and rules that don't feel creative but quietly decide whether your business runs smoothly or becomes fragile.

That's where SKUs and UPCs entered my life—not as abstract concepts, but as friction. At first they felt unnecessary, like something "bigger companies" needed, not small brands building thoughtfully. I assumed platforms would handle it, or that I could circle back later once things took off. Later came sooner than I expected, because once you sell across channels—especially physical products—those identifiers stop being optional. They become the language your systems use to recognize, track, protect, and fulfill what you're selling.

A SKU is how you organize your products internally. A UPC is how the marketplace recognizes them externally. That difference matters more than most people realize. If your SKUs aren't consistent, your reports don't line up. If UPCs aren't handled correctly, listings can break, merge, or get flagged. If neither is thought through, bundles become confusing and fulfillment becomes messy. None of this feels urgent when you're creating. It becomes urgent when you're scaling—even a little.

What caught me off guard was how unforgiving backend mistakes can be. Front-end issues are visible. You notice them. You fix them. Backend issues hide until they create consequences—products showing as "generic," bundles that don't map correctly, inventory that doesn't reconcile, platforms that don't recognize your ownership cleanly. It's not that I didn't care about protection. It's that I didn't know the order of operations yet. And order matters.

This is one of those places where learning by doing can get expensive—not because you're reckless, but because no one really walks you through it in plain language. Most people learn SKUs and UPCs in fragments: a blog post here, a help article there, a forum thread when something breaks.

But what you really need is context.

You need to understand why these things exist. Backend protection isn't about bureaucracy. It's about control—control over how your products are recognized, how they're bundled, how they're fulfilled, and how they scale.

When you skip that layer, you're borrowing stability instead of owning it.

And borrowed stability has limits.

This gets especially real when you start creating bundles. Bundles sound simple—book plus shirt, workbook plus mug, a limited set that feels special. But bundles introduce complexity fast if the backend isn't prepared. Each component needs to be recognized individually. The bundle needs to be recognized as its own product. Inventory needs to know what's being pulled. If that logic isn't clean, bundles become a headache instead of a value-add.

From here, we move into the next layer of protection—because connection gets real when you start building for the long haul.

This is where I want to pause and give you the checklist I wish I had early. Not a technical manual. Not a 40-step setup guide. Just the essentials—the kind of list you can come back to without spiraling. Before you sell a physical product across channels, you should be able to answer five questions without guessing: do you know how each product is identified internally, do you know how each product is identified externally, do you know whether your identifiers are reusable or single-use, do you know how bundles are structured and tracked, and do you know who owns the listing—not just who fulfills it.

That's it. Five questions. If you can answer those clearly, you're in a good place. If you can't, it doesn't mean you're behind. It means you've reached the point where backend protection matters.

This is also where mindset comes into play. It's easy to feel embarrassed when you realize there are things you didn't know. It's easy to think you "should have figured it out sooner." But that mindset doesn't help you build better systems. Curiosity does. Because this is the season where you shift from getting it out there… to making it sustainable. And sustainable doesn't mean rigid. It means resilient.

A protected backend allows you to experiment on the front end without fear. It lets you test offers, try bundles, and expand channels without constantly worrying that one misstep will unravel everything. That peace is worth more than speed. And this is where the theme of connection shows up again. When products are protected on the backend, your systems can talk to each other. Orders flow cleanly. Reporting makes sense. Fulfillment becomes predictable. And your energy goes back where it belongs—into serving customers and refining your message.

This is one of those chapters that feels unglamorous until you live it. But once you've lived it, you don't want to build without it. Because backend protection isn't about control for control's sake. It's about stewardship—stewardship of your work, stewardship of your time, stewardship of what you're building for the long haul. And if there's one thing this entire book keeps coming back to, it's this: clarity creates freedom. Protecting your backend gives you clarity, and clarity gives you room to breathe.

PART III

Bring It Home

This is the part where I stop trying to sound impressive and just tell the truth. Because if MarketABLE taught me anything, it's that quiet doesn't mean you're behind. Sometimes quiet means you're becoming. Sometimes it's the pause where God is rebuilding something in you—something sturdy enough to actually hold what you've been asking Him for. The older I get, the more I realize I don't need momentum as much as I need stability. I don't need hype as much as I need peace. And I definitely don't need a business that looks good online but feels shaky behind the scenes.

I'm not turning this into a legal or tax manual, because I'm not one. But I will say this: the best peace of mind I ever bought was clarity.

Not the flashy kind—the boring kind.

The kind you get when you finally understand what your state expects, what deadlines exist, what fees repeat every year, and what actually happens if you miss them. That kind of clarity doesn't make you feel "boss babe." It makes you feel safe.

And the truth is, connected marketing works better when your business foundation is stable, because the stress of "am I even set up right?" will quietly sabotage everything else. You can have a great offer, a clean message, and a content plan you actually like—and still stall out because there's a low-grade panic humming in the background.

That panic doesn't always show up like fear. Sometimes it looks like procrastination. Sometimes it looks like picking at your website again. Sometimes it looks like redesigning something that didn't need redesigning. Sometimes it looks like overthinking social media because posting feels easier than dealing with the real-world admin that makes you feel exposed. And if you've ever been there, I'm not judging you. I'm just naming it, because I've lived it. There's a specific kind of exhaustion that comes from trying to build a brand while secretly wondering if you're one missed filing away from a mess you don't even understand.

Then there's the admin reality nobody puts on the highlight reel: sales tax, use tax, quarterly filings, annual reports, and the "Do I still file if I didn't sell anything?" questions that show up the moment you decide to do business the right way. It's not glamorous, but it's part of staying legit. And honestly, it's one more reason small business owners feel overloaded.

You're not just building a brand—you're building a compliant entity while the world still expects you to post content like you've got a full team.

That disconnect is real, and it's a big part of why people feel like they're failing when they're actually just carrying too much.

So this section is about bringing it home. Not just to the website and the tools and the content, but to real life. To the part where you create stability on purpose. To the part where you stop avoiding the unsexy pieces because you finally see they're not punishment—they're protection. To the part where you build in a way that lets you breathe, lets you lead, and lets you stay honest with yourself about what you can carry in this season. Because when the foundation is stable, the system can actually do what it was designed to do. It can hold you. And you can stop building like you're one surprise away from collapsing.

And if you ever bring in help—contractors, a VA, a developer—backend protection means boundaries around access. Give the access they need, not the access you forget you gave. Your business can be collaborative and still be secured. That balance is part of building something that lasts.

Protection also means records. Even if you're not a numbers person, you deserve to know what's coming in, what's going out, and what you owe. That doesn't require a finance degree. It requires one simple system for receipts, one place for income tracking, and a monthly habit of checking in. The goal is confidence, not perfection.

Protection is one of those words that sounds serious until you've lost something you can't easily get back. A product isn't just a product once people start buying it. It becomes a promise. It becomes reputation. It becomes income you're counting on. And that means the back end has to be protected the same way you protect the front end.

One of the most practical shifts I made was thinking in terms of 'keys.' Who has the keys to your domain, your website, your email list, your payment processor, your social accounts, your Google business profile? If the answer is 'someone else,' that's not a partnership—it's vulnerability. Even if you trust the person, your business shouldn't depend on their continued availability to stay alive.

This is where documentation becomes a form of protection too. Logins stored safely. Renewal dates tracked. Subscriptions reviewed. A simple list of accounts and access points. It sounds boring until you need it, and then it feels like relief. Because the goal isn't to remember everything. The goal is to be able to find what you need when you need it.

Backend protection also includes customer protection. Clear confirmation emails. Clear delivery steps. Clear support channels. When those pieces are missing, customers feel uncertain, and uncertainty creates refunds, complaints, and bad reviews. Most customer problems aren't about the product—they're about confusion in the path.

So if you're building products right now, don't wait until you're overwhelmed to protect the backend. Start with ownership, access, and one clean system of record. That's how you build something that can grow without constantly putting you back in crisis mode.

Stable beats flashy every time. Next: "Trademarks and IP Without Panic".

CHAPTER 22

Trademarks and IP Without Panic

I didn't wake up one day and decide I wanted to learn trademarks—I learned them the way most small business owners do: the moment I realized the name I was building could outgrow my ability to "just wing it."

There's a point in business where you realize you're not only selling products or services anymore. You're protecting meaning. You're protecting language people repeat. You're protecting frameworks you've poured your time into. And suddenly the thing that felt like branding starts to feel like identity—because it is.

The tricky part is that trademarks and intellectual property can sound like "big business talk" until you're staring at a very real moment of pressure. You've built the offer. You've used the name publicly. You've invested in the website, the domain, the materials, the social handles. People are starting to associate the thing with you. And then it hits you: if someone else uses it, you don't just lose a word—you lose clarity. You lose trust. You lose traction. Not because you're dramatic, but because confusion costs real money.

The first time I walked into that world wasn't with B Creative Systems™. It was with SparkleAddies years ago. I remember feeling proud and nervous at the same time—proud because I had built something worth protecting, nervous because the process made everything feel official. It was like the paperwork was asking me, "Are you really going to stand behind this?" And for a small business owner, that can feel bigger than it should.

Later, in my corporate role, I saw the IP world from a different angle. I helped secure new product technology protection and supported work around patents, and that experience shaped the way I think about protection now. It taught me that IP isn't about ego. It's about clarity and ownership in the marketplace. It's about reducing confusion before confusion has the chance to grow legs.

That's why I frame this chapter as "without panic." Because the panic usually isn't about the forms. It's about what the forms represent. They represent commitment. They represent the future. They represent you saying, out loud, "This matters enough to protect."

And if you're a builder, that can trigger a very human spiral: What if I'm too late? What if someone already has it? What if I file wrong and waste money? What if I can't keep up with the deadlines? What if my business shifts and I'm stuck?

Are We Connected?

If you've felt any of that, you're normal. You care. That's all it means.

I'm not an attorney, and this isn't legal advice. This is lived experience and plain-language orientation so you can make better decisions—and ask better questions—without acting like trademarks are a secret society.

Here's the simplest way I hold it: a trademark protects your brand identifier—your name (and sometimes your logo or tagline)—in the category of goods or services you're actually selling, so the market doesn't get confused by someone else using something identical or too close in the same lane.

That "lane" part matters. A trademark isn't a magic force field that protects a word everywhere forever. Protection is scoped. It's tied to what you offer and how you offer it. That's why you can sometimes see the same word used by totally different companies, because they're operating in different categories that don't overlap in a confusing way.

That scope is also why I don't believe in trademarking everything. This is where people start spinning out. They try to trademark every offer name, every package title, every catchy phrase they've ever posted, and suddenly protection becomes a panic response instead of a strategy. Most businesses do better when they protect the core: the brand name, the flagship framework, and the identifying language people associate directly with the business. If you protect the core, the rest can flex without you living in fear.

This is also where the ™ and ® symbols come into play in a way that's more practical than people realize. The ™ symbol is generally used to signal "I'm claiming this as my mark," even if it's not federally registered yet. The ® symbol is only used after a mark is actually registered. That's one of those tiny details that sounds picky until you realize it's one of the fastest ways to accidentally look sloppy when you're trying to look legitimate.

Another piece that trips people up is the difference between intent-to-use and in-use filings. Intent-to-use is you saying, "I'm not selling under this mark yet, but I intend to, and I want to reserve my position." In-use is you saying, "I'm already using this in real commerce, and here is proof." Both can be valid. The difference isn't whether you're real—the difference is timing.

Timing matters because trademarking has a clock. And the clock is where builders start to feel pressure, especially if you're still building the infrastructure around the mark. That's where the specimen comes in. A specimen is basically proof that you're using the mark in real business—not in a logo file, not in a private draft, not in a name you love in your notes app. It's evidence that customers can actually encounter the mark in the way you claimed.

In real life, a specimen can be more practical than people think. It can be a product label or packaging that shows the mark. It can be a website page where the mark is clearly shown next to the goods or services being sold, with a real path to purchase or book. It can be an invoice or sales receipt tied to the mark. The point is that it shows the mark being used in a way that connects to commerce.

If you file intent-to-use, you're not failing if you need more time. Extensions are common. They aren't shameful. They're the system acknowledging what business owners already know: building takes time, and life doesn't always cooperate with timelines.

I used to hear the word "extension" and feel like I was admitting defeat. Now I see it as maturity. It's you saying, "I'm still building. I'm still committed. I'm doing this responsibly."

Another practical guardrail that saves a lot of heartache is this: don't fall in love with a name without doing a basic search first. It doesn't have to be obsessive. It's just wise. A quick check can tell you whether you're stepping into an obvious conflict before you invest money and identity into a word that's already taken in your lane.

And even beyond the legal side, the trademark process forces something helpful: it forces clarity. It makes you define what you actually sell. It makes you choose your category. It makes you stop trying to be everything. That clarity spills into marketing because precision creates connection. People understand you faster. They trust you faster. They know what you're about.

Trademarks also teach you something bigger than paperwork: they teach you the difference between building for attention and building for legacy. Attention wants speed. Legacy requires structure.

But I also want to name what's real. Sometimes you file, and then life changes. Sometimes a developer leaves. Sometimes funding doesn't come through. Sometimes a project pauses. Sometimes you realize the vision needs realignment. That doesn't mean you were wrong to file. It means you're living. Building is not linear, and trademarks can make that reality feel more intense because they put your vision on a timeline.

This is where faith and strategy meet for me in a very practical way. Protection is wise, but panic is not. You can protect what matters while still giving yourself room to build at the pace your life can sustain. You can file extensions without shame. You can adjust without pretending. You can hold integrity even while you're still becoming.

Because the goal isn't just to "own" a trademark on paper. The goal is to own your lane with confidence—so your message isn't constantly diluted by confusion, and your business can grow without you looking over your shoulder.

If you're reading this and thinking, I'm behind, I waited too long, I don't even know where to start—breathe. Start with the core. Start with what truly represents your brand. Start with clarity. Then move forward one decision at a time. Protection isn't supposed to steal your peace. It's supposed to support what you're building.

And once the core is protected—or at least intentionally being protected—something shifts. You get to build louder, cleaner, and more confidently, because you're not just creating in the moment. You're building something that can last.

That's a perfect setup for the next chapter, because publishing works the same way. It's not just creation—it's structure, distribution, identifiers, and clarity that turns your message into an asset that keeps working even when you're not "on."

CHAPTER 23

Publishing as Marketing

I used to think publishing was a completely separate world from "small business." Like a gated neighborhood for people with literary degrees, big followings, or a perfectly linear story. Publishing felt like something you did after you were already established—after your life was tidy, your brand was polished, and your message was fully formed.

But real life is not linear. Healing isn't either. And for me, books didn't begin as a marketing plan. They began as a place to put what I was carrying. Writing became the thing that helped me name what was true, sort what was messy, and turn lived experience into something useful—something that could help someone else too. The marketing came later, almost like a byproduct, and it surprised me how powerful that byproduct became.

Because a book does something a post can't. A post introduces you. A reel gets attention. A website legitimizes you. But a book holds someone. It holds attention longer than a scroll allows. It holds the questions people don't know how to ask yet. It gives your ideas room to land. And in a small business world where trust is everything, a book becomes quiet authority that doesn't require you to keep performing for visibility every day.

That's also where AIfficiency™ shows up in this story, because the result people notice isn't only the books themselves—it's the momentum behind them. Six books in one year still surprises me when I say it out loud, not because it's a flex, but because it's evidence that something shifted. I didn't become a different person overnight. I didn't suddenly love every part of the process. I became supported. I became clearer. I became more consistent. And AI helped reduce the drag between what I knew and what I could actually finish.

AIfficiency™, the way I mean it, isn't "AI did it for me." It's that AI reduced friction. It helped me outline faster, organize cleaner, revise without spiraling, and stay in motion without getting swallowed by overwhelm. The efficiency wasn't just speed. It was follow-through. It was the difference between "I have this idea" and "this is now a real asset someone can buy, read, and be helped by."

And when I say "six books," I don't mean just one kind of book. I mean my actual body of work in the order it unfolded: Momma Knows Best, The Uncommon AffAIr, Prompt Therapy: The Uncommon Affair with AI, The Uncommon AffAIr with AI Prompt Therapy Workbook, MarketABLE, and now Are We Connected? Each one came from a different place in me, and each one serves a different purpose. Some are story-first, some are framework-first, and some are soul-first. But together, they created something I didn't fully realize I was building at the time: an ecosystem people could enter through multiple doors.

That's the marketing part, even when you don't call it that. Most small business owners hear "marketing" and immediately think content—like it's your job to constantly feed the internet so it doesn't forget you exist. Content matters, but content is not the same thing as an asset. Content is often disposable. An asset keeps working while you're living your real life. And books—when they're connected to a clear path—are one of the most underrated trust-building assets a business owner can create.

But publishing isn't just writing. Writing is the heart work. Publishing is the system work. Publishing is formats, files, trim sizes, margins, metadata, categories, keywords, edition management, proof copies, and whole lot of patience. Publishing is understanding that what looks great on your screen can print slightly off if you don't respect the technical side. Publishing is learning that "done" has layers: manuscript done, interior file done, cover file done, upload done, proof approved, listing optimized, and then public.

If you don't know that going in, publishing can become another one of those small business traps where you're doing good work in a messy way that creates unnecessary stress. One of the most helpful shifts I ever made was separating author mode from publisher mode. Author mode is where you write like a human. You tell the truth. You shape meaning. You build the message. Publisher mode is where you respect the machine. You think in specs. You consider the reader's experience. You make sure the book is legible, printable, and findable.

And if you're doing this as a small business owner, there's a third layer too: marketer mode. That's where you decide what role the book plays in your ecosystem and what you want it to do. Because a book can be art, and it can still have a job. It can be a front door. A credibility anchor. A lead generator. A referral tool. A speaking asset. A nurture piece. A product. A bridge into what you offer next. But it only becomes that when you connect it on purpose instead of letting it float out there like a beautiful island with no path back to you.

This is where the practical pieces matter, and I want to give them to you the way I would have wanted someone to give them to me: simple, clear, and not overwhelming. Start by understanding formats, because formats shape the reader's experience and they shape your workload. Paperback is the most common starting point. Hardcover is a different build. An eBook is not just a copy-and-paste of your print file—it has to function across devices and screen sizes. Audio is its own lane entirely, with its own production process and its own decisions around distribution.

Then there's the physical reality people don't think about until they're staring at a cover template: the spine. Spine width isn't aesthetic. It's math. It's determined by trim size, page count, and paper type. That means when your interior changes, your spine can change. When your spine changes, your cover file changes. This is normal, but it's one of the reasons publishing requires patience and sequencing. You don't finalize your cover until your interior is stable enough to stop shifting.

Proofing matters more than people want it to. You need to see it printed. Not just once. A screen is forgiving and print is honest. Proofing is where you catch the little things that can quietly undermine the quality of the experience—spacing, margins, page breaks, headers, chapter openings, and cover alignment. It's also where you decide if the book feels like a real product in someone's hands, not just words you wrote.

Identifiers matter too, even if you don't love acronyms. The systems care about identifiers whether we do or not. Amazon has its own identifiers. ISBNs are universal identifiers that can be used across channels. If you're keeping your distribution inside one ecosystem, the simplest route can be enough. If you want wide distribution, you need to think differently about identifiers, editions, and where your book is being listed. And if you choose programs that increase visibility inside one platform, it's important to understand what you're trading for that visibility, because sometimes visibility comes with exclusivity.

Metadata is another layer most people underestimate. Metadata is the structured information that tells the marketplace what your book is and who it's for. Title, subtitle, description, categories, keywords, author name, series name, imprint—those things create the map. A map for the algorithm, yes, but also a map for a human trying to decide if this book is for them. Metadata isn't about tricking anyone. It's about being findable, and being findable is a form of service.

Publishing also creates legitimacy faster than most marketing tactics, and I didn't fully understand that until I experienced it. People treat you differently when you're an author, not because being an author makes you superior, but because it signals follow-through. It signals depth. It signals that you can hold an idea long enough to complete it. In a world where everyone is posting fragments, a book signals cohesion. And cohesion builds trust.

But publishing will also reveal the gaps in your ecosystem. Because once your book exists, people will look for the next step. They'll search your name. They'll click your website. They'll look for what you offer.

They'll look for a path. If the book is strong but the path is messy, you'll feel it immediately. That's why publishing as marketing only works when it's connected.

Connected doesn't mean you send people ten different directions. It means you give them one clear place to go next. One link. One page. One invitation. One next step that feels like a handrail instead of a maze. The goal isn't to overwhelm someone with your ecosystem. The goal is to give them a path into it.

And that's why this chapter belongs in Are We Connected? Because publishing is one of the clearest examples of what happens when you build something that can carry your message without requiring you to be on-stage every day. A book can be quiet marketing. It can be steady marketing. It can be the kind of marketing that builds trust while you're living your real life.

Most small business owners aren't trying to go viral. They're trying to be stable. They're trying to be seen by the right people and supported by systems that make sense. Publishing can be part of that stability when you treat it like a connected asset instead of a standalone accomplishment. When you do, the book stops being "just a book" and becomes a bridge—into your message, your method, your offers, and your bigger ecosystem.

You don't have to publish to be legitimate. But if you do publish, don't just write—connect it. Give it a job. Give the reader a clear next step. Let the work you poured into those pages keep working for you long after launch week fades.

Because the marketing isn't supposed to drain you. It's supposed to carry your message farther than you can carry it alone. And when you build publishing with connection in mind, it can.

CHAPTER 24
Money/Admin Reality

Entrepreneurship gets sold like freedom. And it is, sometimes. But nobody sells the part where freedom comes with receipts, renewals, reports, passwords, and paperwork that doesn't care how creative you are. You can be brilliant at your craft and still feel like your business is one missed deadline away from embarrassment.

I don't say that dramatically. I say it because I've lived it. I've watched administrative overwhelm quietly kill momentum, not because people weren't talented, but because their systems weren't connected enough to support growth.

Nobody starts a business because they're excited about administration. No one wakes up with a little thrill in their chest thinking, I can't wait to track, file, categorize, renew, reconcile, and prove I'm legitimate today. People start businesses because they have a gift, a skill, a vision, a service, a product, a fire. They start because they want freedom and impact, and maybe they want flexibility too—because real life is happening at the same time. They start because they want to build something that belongs to them. And then, somewhere between the first sale and the first "this is actually working," you run into the part of business nobody puts on the highlight reel: the part that decides whether your business can hold its own weight.

It's not glamorous. It's not cute. It's not the part you post about. It's the part that shows up as, Where did that charge come from? Why is this payment not matching that invoice? Which login did I use for this? Where did I put that receipt? When is that renewal? Who has access to our accounts? What is actually due—and what did I miss because I didn't know it existed? That kind of stress doesn't feel like marketing stress. It feels like the floor moving under you. And for me, this is my least favorite part of the whole deal.

I can bounce back and forth between PC and Mac without thinking twice. I can speak creative and technical. I can understand how systems should connect, how they should flow, how they should reduce friction and create clarity. I'm not intimidated by complexity—until the complexity looks like spreadsheets and balance sheets. Living in that world makes my soul want to leave my body. There's a reason I didn't finish my minor in business, and it wasn't because I couldn't handle the workload. It was because of that dang financial accounting class. The one where everything is numbers, and everything matters, and your brain has to stay inside the lines for long periods of time without wandering off into creativity. I remember thinking, Who is this for? Who wakes up excited to do this? I know some people do, and God bless them, but it just wasn't me, and if I'm being honest, it still isn't.

What I learned the grown-up way, the business-owner way, is that if you want to make money, you have to manage the money. And if you want peace, you have to respect the administrative side of what you're building, because ignoring it doesn't make it go away. It just makes it louder later. Most people don't get overwhelmed because they're irresponsible. They get overwhelmed because they're building in real life. They're doing the service, running operations, answering customers, handling family stuff, trying to market, trying to stay consistent, trying to stay afloat, and the backend becomes something you "handle later" until later turns into a mess.

The mess is rarely one dramatic moment. It's death by a thousand tiny things. It's a subscription you forgot you signed up for. It's a charge you don't recognize, but it's "only $18," so you let it go. It's a free trial that quietly became an annual plan. It's an invoice you meant to send that never got sent. It's a payment that came in, but you don't remember what it was for. It's a deposit that hits, but the paperwork doesn't match. It's a receipt you swear you saved somewhere. It's a login tied to a personal email because you were moving fast when you set it up. It's a second tool you bought because the first tool was never fully set up. It's a third tool because you were tired and needed something to be easier. It's a fourth tool because a guru said you "had" to have it. None of it feels catastrophic in the moment, but stacked together, it creates a constant background hum of stress, and that hum makes you feel behind even when things are going well.

This is one of the reasons I'm so passionate about connected systems. Not because I'm obsessed with tools, but because I've watched administrative chaos quietly kill momentum. Momentum dies when your brain is carrying too much. It dies when you can't see what you're spending, when you can't tell what you're actually making, when you don't know what's due, when you can't find what you need, and when everything is scattered across emails, logins, apps, and "I'll remember it." You don't need to become an accountant to fix this. You don't need to turn into a numbers person overnight. You don't need to build a corporate finance department in your spare bedroom. You do need a foundation that isn't held together by memory and crossed fingers, because the admin side of business is what makes your business legible—not just to the IRS, not just to a bank, not just to a grant program, but to you.

The administrative side is the structure that keeps the business from living only inside your head. It's the separation, the access, the organization, the "where does this live and who can touch it" layer. It's what keeps your business from feeling like a pile of loose papers and random logins that only you can decode. One of the simplest and most underrated moves you can make is separation, and I don't mean separation as a fancy upgrade. I mean separation as protection. Separate accounts when you can. Separate business spending from personal spending. Separate business logins from the random personal email you used in a hurry. Separate access so the right people can find what they need and you're not the single point of failure for everything. It doesn't have to be perfect to be progress, but it does have to be intentional, because when everything is mixed, you can't see what's real, and when you can't see what's real, you can't lead.

Admin also needs rhythm. I know "rhythm" can sound soft, but it's one of the strongest things you can build into your business. Overwhelm happens when admin only gets attention in crisis mode, when something breaks or something is due or something becomes delinquent, and then you drop everything, scramble, and promise yourself you'll "stay on top of it" next time. A rhythm is what keeps you from living like that. A rhythm can be as simple as one consistent weekly check-in, not a dramatic overhaul, not an eight-hour "get my life together" day, just a recurring moment where you look at what came in, what went out, what needs attention, what needs to be canceled, what needs to be saved, and what needs a follow-up. A rhythm doesn't make you perfect. It makes you steady, and steadiness is what creates peace.

The money side is where things get emotional fast, because money isn't just numbers. Money is energy and pressure and responsibility and possibility, and it's also the quickest way to expose what's disconnected, because when the money doesn't make sense, everything feels unstable. You don't need a finance degree to manage the money side of your business, but you do need visibility. Visibility means you can answer basic questions without panic. How much did we bring in this month? How much went out? What did it go to? What subscriptions are we carrying? What's recurring and what's one-time? What is the actual profit after the noise is removed? A lot of business owners avoid these questions because they're afraid of the answers, but avoiding the numbers doesn't protect you. It just delays the moment you have to face them, and it makes the fear bigger than the reality.

This is also where subscriptions and tool stacks become more than just "cost of doing business." They're not harmless. They're quiet. They hide. They stack. They renew. They stay on autopilot while you're busy building, and they become background noise in your statements until you sit down and realize you're paying for things you don't use, don't understand, or don't even remember signing up for. And every subscription isn't just money. It's mental load. Every login is a responsibility. Every tool is a

Are We Connected?

relationship you have to maintain. Every platform adds a layer of administration, even if it's small. Every disconnected tool creates more work. If you're building lean, you can't afford a messy stack, not emotionally and not financially.

That's why the money side and the admin side have to work together, even if you personally hate one of them. Admin without money visibility turns into busywork. Money without admin structure turns into confusion. Together, they create stability, and stability is what gives you the freedom to grow. Growth multiplies everything. More payments mean more tracking. More products mean more categorization. More platforms mean more renewals. More sales channels mean more reporting. If your backend isn't ready, growth starts to feel like punishment instead of reward, and I refuse to romanticize that. You didn't build a business to feel trapped inside it.

Here's the mindset shift that helped me the most: you don't have to love this part. You just have to respect it. Respect looks like keeping your business traceable and calm. It looks like knowing what entity you're operating under and whether you're current. It looks like knowing who has access to what and where the documentation lives. It looks like having a basic system for money flow so you can see reality instead of guessing it. And if you're behind, I want you to hear this clearly: embarrassment is a liar. Embarrassment tells you you're late, you should have known, you're the only one. You're not. Most business owners build first and organize later. The difference between businesses that survive and businesses that stall isn't who never makes a mess. It's who eventually cleans it up.

When you clean it up, something powerful happens. You get brave. Not because you suddenly love spreadsheets, and not because you suddenly become a numbers person, but because you're prepared. Prepared enough to apply for funding without scrambling. Prepared enough to take on a bigger client without fear. Prepared enough to scale without losing your mind. Prepared enough to build more without everything collapsing under the weight. That's the point. A clean backend makes you confident on the front end. It makes you steady. It makes you consistent. It makes follow-through possible, not because you're perfect, but because your business is supported.

So if you do nothing else, do this: make your business legible to you. Make it traceable. Make it calm enough that you're not afraid to look at it. That's the difference between momentum that feels exciting and momentum that feels like punishment. In the next chapter, we'll talk grants, and I'll show you how this same "legible business" idea is exactly what most grant programs are trying to confirm.

CHAPTER 25

Small Business Grants: What They Actually Want

Who is Grant? And how do I get money from him? Because that's honestly what "small business grants" can sound like when you're in the middle of real life—running the business, doing the work, answering customers, handling family stuff, trying to market, trying to stay consistent, trying to remember where that one lead even landed. Grants get talked about like hidden money, like there's a secret list somewhere, and if you just find the right link or say the right words, funding appears. That framing creates more frustration than clarity, because it sets people up to believe grants are about luck—or worse, about worthiness. They're not. And "Grant" isn't your rich uncle with a checkbook. He's a system. A process. A decision made by people whose job is to reduce risk while supporting a mission.

Before we talk about grant readiness, we have to talk about awareness. A lot of small business owners don't even know grants exist—at least not in a real, "this could apply to me" way. Or they've heard the word and mentally file it under nonprofits, cities, schools, or "other people." Some people assume grants are only for women-owned businesses, minority-owned businesses, rural areas, disaster zones, tech startups, or nonprofits. Some assume grants are only for people who already have everything together. Some assume it's a scam because they've seen too many "pay me $297 and I'll get you free money" videos. And some people simply don't have the time to chase something that feels like a long shot when they're already busy trying to keep the lights on.

Here's the truth: grants are real, and the range is wider than most people realize. Some are national. Some are state-level. Some are regional. Some are surprisingly local—tied to your county, your city, your community foundations, local banks, economic development groups, industry associations, and yes, sometimes even your local Chamber of Commerce. Some grants are tied to specific goals: job creation, storefront improvements, equipment, technology, training, marketing, recovery, agriculture, sustainability, innovation, childcare, veteran support, rural development. Some are big checks. Some are small but strategic. Some are one-time. Some are recurring. Some require a match. Some don't. Some are meant to help you start. Some are meant to help you stabilize. Some are meant to help you scale.

That's why I don't like the myth that grants are "free money." Nothing is free. Grants come with requirements—applications, documentation, timelines, and sometimes reporting. But "requirements" doesn't mean "impossible." It just means the money is attached to responsibility. And if you can learn what they're actually looking for, grants become less of a mystery and more of a strategy.

This is also where you may hear the phrase "grant writer" and assume that means grants are reserved for professionals and institutions. Grant writers are real. People absolutely make a living doing this. Many nonprofits and large organizations hire them because they're constantly pursuing funding and they have the structure to manage it. But grant writers aren't only for nonprofits, and grants aren't only for organizations with teams. A lot of small business owners apply without one. Some hire help for specific applications. Some work with consultants. Some learn by applying and getting better each round. The skill isn't some magical language. The skill is clarity: explaining what you do, who you serve, what you need, and what will change if you receive support—without exaggerating and without rambling.

That's the core thing I want you to understand: grants are not about how impressive your dream is. Grants are about readiness. I didn't understand that at first. I thought grants were primarily about ideas—big vision, community impact, potential. Those things matter, but they're rarely the deciding factor. What reviewers are really trying to determine is whether your business makes sense on paper. Not perfect sense. Not corporate-level polish. But clear sense. They're asking themselves, "If we put money into this business, will it be used the way it's intended, and will it produce the outcome this grant exists to support?"

Clarity is the currency here. Most grants are designed to reduce risk. They're not trying to fund chaos, even if the chaos is passionate and well-intentioned. They want to see that if money enters your business, it has somewhere sensible to go. They want to understand what you do, who you serve, how you make money—or how you will—and what this funding will actually change. Those questions aren't traps. They're filters. Grants don't want a busy ecosystem. They want a legible one.

Legible means a stranger can read your application and understand your business without you standing there explaining what you meant. Legible means your offer isn't a mystery. Legible means your numbers aren't smoke. Legible means your plan matches your stage. Legible means you're not applying for $25,000 to do fourteen different things that don't connect to each other. It's not about being fancy. It's about being coherent.

When I started looking at grants more seriously, I noticed a pattern. The applications weren't asking for magic. They were asking for basics, just clearly explained: business information, entity details, a short narrative about what you do, a plan for use of funds, a budget, a timeline, sometimes a basic financial snapshot, sometimes proof of revenue, sometimes proof of need, sometimes a story about community impact, sometimes a plan for growth or job creation. Not pages and pages of jargon. Just a business that can be understood.

This is where so many small business owners quietly opt out. They assume grants are only for people who already "have it together," so they don't apply. Or they apply once, get overwhelmed by the paperwork, and decide it's not worth the effort. Or they avoid it because they're embarrassed about what their backend looks like. But grants don't require you to be huge. They require you to be understandable. Understandable businesses feel safer to fund.

And safety isn't about being boring. It's about being specific. Specificity shows thoughtfulness. Specificity shows planning. Specificity shows that you've done more than dream. A vague vision can be inspiring, but it's hard to fund. A clear plan—even a modest one—is easier to support. If your application describes ten initiatives, five platforms, three audiences, and a dozen goals, the reviewer doesn't see ambition. They see diffusion. They wonder which part of this they're actually funding—and whether it will make a measurable difference.

This is one of the most important shifts you can make: grants like focus. They like knowing exactly what the money will be used for and what outcome it's expected to produce. Not because they're rigid, but because they have to justify decisions. A grant program has a purpose. Your job is to show how your request fits that purpose, and how you will carry it responsibly.

So what do grants actually want, in plain language? They want a business that is clear, consistent, and trackable. They want to see that you know what you're doing, even if you're still building. They want to see that you're not trying to use a grant to become a different person overnight. They want to see that you have a plan that matches your capacity. They want to see that the funding will produce something measurable: equipment purchased, training completed, marketing executed, storefront improved, website rebuilt, inventory acquired, employees hired, certifications earned, systems installed, outreach expanded. Measurable doesn't mean you need to guarantee a million dollars in revenue. It means you can articulate what will happen, when it will happen, and why it matters.

They also want stewardship. This is where the money and admin side of business becomes a real factor. A lot of people think grant applications are about telling a good story. They are partly story—but it's a story that has to stand up on paper. Reviewers want to know you can manage money responsibly. That doesn't mean you need a finance degree. It means you need to show that you've thought through what happens after the check clears. How will the funds be tracked? Who oversees spending? What expenses are expected? What's the timeline? What happens when the grant period ends? Funders don't want to light a match and walk away. They want to believe the contribution has lasting impact.

This is exactly where your backend matters. If your business records are scattered, your story becomes harder to tell. If your finances are unclear, your confidence drops. If your entity details are messy, the application process becomes stressful instead of strategic. Clean doesn't mean complicated. It means intentional. It means your business is separated enough that you can speak clearly about it without scrambling. It means you can produce documents when asked without panic. It means you can answer basic questions without guesswork.

This is also where I want to gently call out something that keeps good people stuck: trying to impress instead of explain. Some small business owners assume grant reviewers want big words, big vision, big everything. So they write like a brochure. They write like a pitch to investors. They write like they're trying to prove they deserve it. The irony is, that usually makes an application weaker. Grant reviewers aren't impressed by scale fantasies. They're reassured by traction and intention. Even small traction counts— existing customers, early sales, proof of concept, documented demand, a waiting list, testimonials, community partnerships. Those things tell a story of momentum, not just aspiration.

Here's a practical way to think about it: your application should read like a clear conversation with a smart stranger who wants to help but needs to understand. What do you do? Who do you do it for? Why does it matter? What do you need? What will you do with the funds? What changes after? How will you track it? That's the spine. Everything else is support.

Now let's talk about one more thing people don't realize: not every grant is worth applying for. Some grants don't align with your stage. Some don't align with your mission. Some come with reporting requirements that outweigh the benefit. Some require matching funds you don't have. Some are hyper-competitive and may not be worth your energy right now. Chasing every opportunity can be as draining as chasing every platform. Discernment matters here too. Money always comes with responsibility. Free money still has weight.

The goal isn't to win grants. The goal is to secure support that strengthens what you're already building. That shift changes everything. Instead of asking, "How do I get money?" you ask, "What would actually help me move forward?" That question leads to better decisions—and better applications.

This is also why I love the concept of grant readiness, even for the people who never apply. Grant readiness is business readiness. When you prepare your business to be grant-ready, you're also preparing it to be loan-ready, partnership-ready, vendor-ready, investor-ready, and scale-ready. You're learning how to explain your work clearly, track your progress, and articulate your impact. You're building structure that supports growth without you carrying everything in your head.

And here's the quiet truth: even if you never receive a grant, the process of preparing for one makes your business stronger. It forces you to clarify your offer. It forces you to understand your numbers. It forces you to define your next step. That clarity compounds. It reduces stress. It gives you language. It gives you confidence. It makes your business more legible—not just to a reviewer, but to you.

So if you're reading this thinking, "Okay, but where do I even start?" start small and start honest. Start with one clear offer. One clear next step you'd fund if you were the grant program. One simple explanation of what the money would do. One basic budget. One rough financial snapshot. One place where your documents live so you're not digging through inbox searches and screenshots. You don't need a perfect ecosystem. You need a connected one.

If you want a simple mental checklist, here it is in plain language: be clear about what you do, be specific about what you need, be realistic about what you can execute, and be ready to show proof that your business exists beyond an idea. That's it. That's what "ready" looks like. Not perfect. Not polished. Ready.

Grants stop feeling like a gamble when you treat them like a strategy. And once you understand that grants are less about being chosen and more about being understandable, you start moving differently. You build with clarity. You track with intention. You document as you go. You stop assuming opportunities are reserved for someone else. Because they're not. You just have to become the kind of business that can carry support without collapsing under it.

That's the thread to hold onto here: clarity creates calm, and calm creates follow-through. In the next chapter—"Built to Scale, Forced to Pause"—we'll build the next piece of connection so the system can carry more weight without you carrying it alone.

CHAPTER 26
Built to Scale, Forced to Pause

I didn't start out trying to compete with the giants. I wasn't sitting around plotting how to take on HubSpot, GoHighLevel, Zoho, or any of the names that sound like entire departments and entire budgets. I was trying to solve a real problem I kept watching small businesses live inside—one I had lived inside too. And if I'm honest, I thought this would be a Year 3 move. I thought it was something I'd circle back to once the rest of the foundation felt steady. But Year 1 handed me the keys and I said yes before I fully understood the fuel cost.

That's the part people forget when they hear "app idea." They immediately compare it to the big guys. They picture investor-backed roadmaps and a swarm of developers and a glossy product launch. They don't picture a woman at a kitchen table, trying to connect the dots between what she knows, what she's lived, and what small business owners are drowning in every day. They don't picture how many decisions live behind the screen. They don't picture the quiet weight of building something that has to work even when you're tired, even when life happens, even when you're not "in the mood" to be visionary.

Bline™ wasn't born from ego. It was born from frustration. I kept watching marketing stay disconnected even when people were trying hard. Business owners were signing up for platform after platform, stacking subscriptions like they were stacking solutions, and ending up with more logins and less clarity. They were working, spending, trying, posting, buying the course, hiring the contractor, switching the tool, and still feeling like everything was held together by memory and crossed fingers. I knew what they needed wasn't more tools. They needed connection between the tools they already had.

That thought came in a way that felt almost too bold to say out loud: why not build the thing I wish existed? Why not create a branded app around the B10 Core Automation Method™—a command center that helped small businesses (and even agencies) actually see what was happening across their ecosystem without needing ten dashboards and a second brain? I wasn't imagining myself "taking down" anyone. I was imagining myself serving the people who weren't being served well by complexity.

But the moment you speak a vision out loud, other people attach their fears to it. I remember sharing what I was building with a business mentor. He asked me why, so I told him the problem it solved. I told him that even if I never sold one seat, it would still be a really expensive gift to myself—because I needed it. And he looked at me with that careful, loving tone people use when they're trying to help you not get hurt, and he reminded me I'd be going up against the big guys. Big names. Big budgets. Big teams. And then he said something that stung, even though he didn't mean it cruelly: what would stop them from squashing me like the bug that I am?

I remember just sitting with that for a second, because even though he didn't mean it harshly, it landed. Not because I suddenly doubted my capability, but because I understood his point. The giants aren't scary because they're smarter than you. They're scary because they have resources. They have teams. They have staying power. They can keep something alive once it exists—and that's the part people don't talk about when they're cheering you on for having a big idea.

And still… something in me reached for a different frame. The one that has carried me through more than one season where I wasn't sure I had the footing for the next step: What if I fall? Oh, but my darling, what if you fly? I've always loved butterflies. Not in a trendy, "cute aesthetic" way—in a pay-attention way. The transformation. The timing you can't force. The fact that the thing you become is real even when nobody saw it happening. So when he said "bug," I didn't hear it as an insult. I heard it as a reminder that I wasn't building from a boardroom. I was building from real life. And real life still produces flight.

I knew the answer to his question. Nothing—at least not in the way he meant it. His point wasn't that I was incapable. His point was that scale has a cost, and the cost isn't just money. It's focus. It's time. It's emotional bandwidth. It's support. It's being able to keep something alive once it exists.

That conversation didn't kill the vision, but it forced a reckoning. It forced me to ask whether I was building from clarity or from something I was trying to prove. There is a version of entrepreneurship where you're always trying to prove you belong in rooms that weren't built for you. And there is another version where you build what you're called to build with the resources you actually have, in the order that makes sense—even if it's slower. That moment made me slow down enough to learn the difference.

I learned more about SaaS and app development than I ever expected to know. I learned what a development plan actually is beyond a dreamy list of features. I learned how UX and UI professionals think and why so much of an app isn't code—it's experience. I learned how automation specialists approach logic and workflow, and why "simple" on the front end can be complicated behind the scenes. I learned what validation really means, and it wasn't the motivational poster version. Validation isn't just "Will people like it?" It's "Will people pay for it consistently at a price that can support the cost of maintaining it?"

That's where the fantasy breaks if you're not careful. Apps aren't one-time builds. They come with monthly hosting fees, database costs, maintenance, security, updates, bug fixes, contractor time, and problems you can't plan for until you're living inside them. If you've never built something like this, it's easy to assume an app is like a website—a project you finish and then move on. It isn't. An app is a living thing. It needs care. It needs infrastructure. It needs attention. And attention costs money.

Somewhere along the way, someone said a sentence that felt like a throwaway comment at the time and later felt like a flashing sign: you don't put your own money into app building. You get funding for that. It hit me like… oh. That's the game. That's what I missed. Because I wasn't building inside the venture world. I was building inside my world—the world where you bootstrap, reinvest, stay scrappy, and try to be wise. The world where you put your own money back into your business because you believe in what you're building and you're trying to do it with integrity.

By the time that reality landed, I had already poured time and money into the ecosystem—into the frameworks, the offerings, the brand, the assets, the books, the structure. I was building a whole house, and then I decided to build a power plant behind it too. And I didn't have the funding pipeline for a power plant. That's the honest truth.

What makes this story harder is that it wasn't a total failure. In some ways, I did something right from the beginning that a lot of people don't do. The foundation was designed to scale. The structure was built with multi-tenancy in mind, which simply means the architecture could support individual businesses, portfolios, and even agency management without needing a complete rebuild later. I wasn't building a one-off tool. I was building something that could expand. Bline™ was meant to be a connected hub built around the B10 Core Automation Method™—a place to capture leads, organize contacts, automate follow-up, and actually see what was working across the system.

The vision was phase-based, modular, and designed to grow with the business, not trap the business. It was meant to serve the owner who just needs the system to run and the team managing multiple brands who needs a broader view. I was building toward that even while I was still learning the language and the economics of SaaS.

And then reality hit the way it usually does in early builds: not as one dramatic explosion, but as a slow unraveling of trust. I worked with a contractor who overpromised and underdelivered. The timeline sounded reasonable. The updates sounded confident. The language sounded like forward movement. And then it became delays, gaps, missed deliverables, and pieces that looked "almost done" but weren't actually functional.

I wasn't left with nothing, but I wasn't left with a finished product either. The build sat in that painful middle space where enough work had been done to make quitting feel like wasting everything, and enough work remained to make finishing feel risky. That is a unique kind of tension, especially when you're funding it yourself. You can't unspend the money. You can't unlearn what you learned. You can't pretend you didn't have the vision. But you also can't ignore the reality of ongoing cost and uncertainty.

While the build was sitting unfinished, the trademark side of the story became real too, because when you're building something branded, you're not just dreaming. You're filing. You're documenting. You're protecting the name as you go. And trademarks don't care about contractor problems. They care about use, timing, and proof. So we did what you do when life hits the timeline: we adjusted the filing posture to match reality and prepared for extensions where needed. Not because the vision died, but because the product wasn't fully live the way it needed to be.

That's where the pause happened. Not a dramatic shutdown. Not a public announcement. A forced pause. Because sometimes pausing isn't a lack of ambition—it's a decision to stop bleeding resources while you get clear about the next right step. The infrastructure isn't abandoned, but it's not being force-fed either. The webpage can be ready. The vision can be documented. The foundation can exist. And it can still be wise to stop and breathe.

The hardest part of a pause like that is the silence it creates. When you're not pushing, you can finally hear the real questions underneath the momentum. Is this aligned? Not aligned with my ego. Not aligned with what would impress people. Aligned with what I'm actually called to carry in this season. Aligned with the order my life can sustain. Aligned with the resources I actually have, not the resources I wish I had.

I don't pretend to know yet what Bline™ will become in the final version of my story. But I know what it already gave me, and it wasn't nothing. It gave me wisdom about the cost of scale. It gave me respect for sequence. It made me see how easily ambition can outrun infrastructure. It taught me that big visions don't just require talent—they require strategy. They require funding. They require support. And if you don't have a funding plan, you end up trying to pay for scale with your own life. That's not noble. That's dangerous.

If you're a small business owner dreaming of tech, this is what I'd tell you from lived experience: validate before you build. Learn the economics before you fall in love with the idea. Build the funnel before you build the platform. And if you still want to build it, don't shame yourself for needing funding. Funding isn't weakness. Funding is structure. Structure is what allows big visions to become real without destroying the builder.

I also had to reframe the story I was telling myself about the pause, because it's easy to label any interruption as failure. But what if it wasn't a failure at all? What if it was the most hands-on business course I've ever taken? Not the kind you enroll in and watch from the sidelines, but the kind you live inside. The kind that teaches you by requiring you to build, adjust, learn, and try again in real time. The kind that doesn't just hand you frameworks, but forces you to develop discernment—because there is no other way forward.

I didn't just learn about app development. I learned about scale, funding, timing, limits, and what I'm willing to carry. Those lessons weren't cheap in the most literal sense, but they were formative in a way no course, certification, or book could have been. When you build something yourself, the learning sticks. You feel the weight of decisions. You learn the cost of shortcuts. You gain respect for the things that look simple from the outside but are complex underneath.

If this was tuition, it was paid in full. And I didn't just walk away with knowledge—I walked away with discernment. Discernment is what helps you keep building without forcing. It's what helps you pause without quitting. It's what helps you hold a vision without letting it eat you alive. Some things don't need to be abandoned. They need to be sequenced. And sometimes the most powerful move you can make is to stop long enough to let wisdom catch up to ambition.

CHAPTER 27
The Busy Ecosystem Trap

Busyness has a weird way of pretending it's progress. You can be doing a lot and still feel stuck, and that's usually the first clue you're not dealing with a motivation problem—you're dealing with a connection problem. The busy ecosystem trap isn't about laziness, and it isn't about not trying hard enough. It's the moment when your business looks alive from the outside, but on the inside you feel like you're constantly moving and rarely arriving.

At some point, every small business owner crosses an invisible line. On one side, you're building, learning, experimenting, trying things on. It's messy, but it feels hopeful. On the other side, you're busy—not productive-busy, not purposeful-busy, just... busy. Your days are full, but nothing feels finished. Your tools are active, but nothing feels connected. Your brand looks like it's doing something, but your results feel oddly flat. That's the trap: activity replaces intention, and motion starts masquerading as momentum.

I've lived there. Most people don't fall into this because they're careless; they fall into it because they're trying to be responsible. They add a tool to solve a problem. They open a platform because someone said they should. They create an offer because opportunity feels urgent. They layer systems because growth feels imminent. Each decision makes sense on its own, but collectively it creates noise—so much noise that you can't hear what's actually working.

This is how businesses end up with five platforms, three audiences, multiple offers, overlapping tools, and no clear path for a customer to follow. Everything is technically "running," but nothing is running together. You're posting, launching, answering, updating, improving... and still feeling like you're starting over every week. The worst part is that it can look impressive to everyone else. From the outside, you seem like you're doing all the things. From the inside, it feels heavy.

Heavy is a signal. Heavy usually means something is misaligned—not broken, just misaligned. The pieces aren't talking to each other. The effort isn't compounding. The energy you're spending isn't returning value in proportion to what it costs you in time, money, and mental load. That's usually when people double down instead of stepping back, because slowing down feels dangerous when you're already tired. But more rarely fixes confusion. Clarity does.

Clarity pulls you out of the busy ecosystem trap, but clarity requires honesty. You have to be willing to look at what you've built and ask questions that don't flatter you. What is actually driving revenue? What is actually serving customers well? What is actually necessary right now—not someday, not in theory, not once your life is calmer. Right now. This is where many businesses realize they're carrying things they don't need: tools they signed up for and never implemented, channels they feel obligated to maintain, offers that made sense once but don't fit anymore. None of that means you failed. It means you evolved.

Evolution requires pruning. Pruning can feel like loss, especially when you invested time and money and hope into a thing, but it's really refinement. You're not tearing down your business—you're clearing space so what matters can grow stronger. One of the most helpful shifts I made was changing how I evaluate decisions. Instead of asking, "Does this sound good?" I started asking, "Does this connect?" Because connection is what makes your effort multiply.

Does this tool connect to the rest of the system, or does it create one more login and one more place for information to get lost? Does this offer connect to a customer journey, or is it a standalone product that leaves people wondering what to do next? Does this platform connect to a clear next step, or does it just create content pressure with no payoff? If the answer is no, the thing might still be good—but it might not be right for now. That distinction matters because good things can still be distracting, and helpful things can still be premature. The busy ecosystem trap thrives on "almost useful."

Here's a practical way to spot it: if you can't answer the question "Where does a new customer go next?" in one sentence, your ecosystem is probably busy. And "go next" doesn't mean "follow me on Instagram, join my email list, read my blog, watch my YouTube, click my Linktree, and schedule a call." It means one clear step. One path. One door. If people have to decide between six doors, most won't choose any of them.

Another way to spot it is friction. Friction is what happens when your systems fight each other instead of supporting each other. You feel it when you're copying and pasting the same information into multiple places, manually fixing what should be automatic, or answering the same questions repeatedly because the path isn't clear. Friction drains creative energy faster than long hours ever could. You can be strong, hardworking, and disciplined, and still feel exhausted if your business requires constant translation between tools and tasks that don't line up.

This is also where identity gets tangled in busyness. When you've worked hard, learned a lot, and invested time and money, letting go can feel personal. You don't want to admit something didn't work. You don't want to waste effort. You don't want to look inconsistent. But changing your mind isn't instability. It's leadership. Leaders adjust when reality changes. Small business owners don't need to lock themselves into every decision forever—they need permission to iterate with intention, not endlessly without direction.

An ecosystem isn't everything you've ever built. An ecosystem is a set of connected elements that support one another. Connection is the defining feature—not quantity. A small ecosystem that works is more powerful than a large one that doesn't. When your ecosystem is connected, your marketing points somewhere. Your sales process makes sense. Your systems reduce effort instead of adding it. Your admin supports growth instead of stalling it. When it's busy, attention is scattered. Follow-through slips. Confidence drops. Fatigue sets in. And fatigue isn't always about workload. Sometimes it's about the constant mental tab-switching required to hold a disconnected business together.

Connected systems don't have to be perfect. They just have to be coherent. They allow you to grow without rebuilding everything every time you change direction. They create visibility so you can see what's working and what isn't without guessing. They give you breathing room, and breathing room is where strategy lives. Without it, every decision feels reactive. With it, you can choose deliberately.

If you're reading this and realizing your ecosystem feels crowded, scattered, or heavier than it needs to be, that's not failure. It's feedback. It's a sign you've reached the point where refinement matters more than expansion. You're not starting over. You're editing. And editing is where good work becomes great.

The busy ecosystem trap isn't something you avoid forever—it's something you learn to recognize faster. The goal isn't to never get busy. The goal is to notice when busy stops serving you, reconnect the pieces that matter most, and make the next step obvious again—for you and for the people you're trying to serve. When connection returns, clarity returns. When clarity returns, momentum stops feeling like chaos and starts feeling like direction.

CHAPTER 28
Faith-Led Alignment

This whole ecosystem has been faith-led—not performative faith, not "perfect Christian business" faith, just the kind of faith that shows up when you're building in real time and you keep choosing peace over panic, truth over image, and connection over chaos. It won't make sense to everyone, and it doesn't have to. Some people will only see the pivots, the brands, the books, the frameworks, the pauses, and the "why would you do it that way?" questions. They'll want a linear story with a clean strategy and a predictable timeline, but that's not how this season was written. This season was led.

The sweet spot—the place where it all overlaps—is where my heart finally resides: healed, happy, and steady. Not because everything went perfectly, but because I stopped building from performance and started building from alignment. That's what I had to learn the hard way: when the system is connected, the builder can breathe. When the builder can breathe, decisions get clearer. When decisions get clearer, momentum becomes sustainable.

Connected doesn't mean complicated. Connected means held—held by structure, held by truth, held by the kind of guidance you can't always explain, but you recognize when you feel it. It means your business isn't riding on adrenaline, and your life isn't paying the price for your ambition.

So if you're reading this and your business feels loud, scattered, or heavy, I want you to know something: you don't have to understand every platform. You don't have to master every tool. You don't have to hustle yourself into burnout to prove you're serious. You just have to come back to what's true, and build from there—one steady step at a time. And if it doesn't make sense to everyone, let it. It only has to make sense to the One leading you—and the people you're called to serve.

I also want to name something that matters, because I know how these seasons feel. Sometimes building looks like nothing. Sometimes you write the guides, build the frameworks, learn the tools, map the system, do the work... and still feel like you're standing in the same place financially. And people—sometimes even people close to you—look at the gap between what you've built and what you've earned and decide that means you aren't good enough. But the gap doesn't prove you're a fraud. It proves you're in the middle. And being in the middle doesn't mean you stop. It means you keep going with your integrity intact.

I jumped ship not because I was pushed, but because I knew staying would cost me more than leaving. When I try to explain that season, I use my own picture for it: leaving something stable and impressive—like stepping off a yacht—and landing in something smaller, lighter, and unfamiliar—like a sailboat—where you realize you're still moving forward, but now you have to learn how to steer differently. That's what building can feel like. That's what marketing can feel like. And if you don't have a foundation, every gust becomes a crisis.

So the work you're doing—whether you're building from scratch, rebuilding after a setback, or simply trying to get organized—matters more than you think. Because you're not just learning tactics. You're learning how to steer. This book wasn't written to make you chase trends. It was written to give you a foundation—something steady, something connected, something you can maintain even when life gets real.

If I could leave you with one clean takeaway from this whole story, it would be this: connection protects the builder.

When your tools are connected, you waste less time. When your message is connected, you second-guess less. When your money and admin are connected, you stop living in fear of what you might have missed. And when your faith is connected to your decisions, you can move without performing. That kind of connection doesn't make life perfect—but it makes building sustainable.

So wherever you are right now—early, messy, rebuilding, pausing, or finally gaining traction—don't measure your business by how loud it looks. Measure it by how clearly it works. Choose one next connected step. Protect the core. Keep your integrity. And let your systems carry what they were meant to carry.

This isn't the end of your story. It's the moment you stop building alone.

About the Author

Brittany P. Webb is a marketing strategist, systems builder, and author who helps small business owners turn scattered marketing into connected digital foundations they can actually maintain. Before launching B Creative Systems™, Brittany spent years leading marketing and communications in fast-paced, high-growth environments, reporting directly to executive leadership through major brand and growth initiatives.

That season taught her what many small businesses never get to see up close: marketing works best when the pieces are connected—visibility, lead capture, follow-up, and clean reporting that shows what's working.

Today, she's the creator of the 12.5 Marketing System™ and B10 Core Automation Method™, practical frameworks that simplify the noise in a digital world and helps business owners build online marketing they can understand—whether they DIY it or outsource it with confidence. Brittany lives in Florida with her husband and three children, and she believes the most powerful marketing isn't loud—it's connected, consistent, and built to last.

Connect with Brittany at brittanypwebb.com

www.ingramcontent.com/pod-product-compliance
Lightning Source LLC
Chambersburg PA
CBHW060507030426
42337CB00015B/1788